GREAT GAIN

GLEANED FROM THE WRITINGS
OF
THOMAS BROOKS

Vintage Puritan Series
GLH Publishing
LOUISVILLE, KY

Originally published in 1869 by A. Hislop & Company.
Public Domain

GLH Publishing Reprint, 2021

ISBN:
Paperback 978-1-64863-102-3
Epub 978-1-64863-059-0

*For information on new releases, weekly
deals, and free ebooks visit
www.GLHpublishing.com*

"As a writer, Brooks scatters stars with both his hands:
he hath dust of gold; in his storehouse are all manner of precious stones…. One of these pithy extracts
may assist our meditations for a whole day, and may
open up some sweet passage of Scripture to our understandings; and perhaps some brief sentence may
stick in the sinner's conscience, like an arrow from
the bow of God."

C. H. Spurgeon.

To the Reader.

Honest Reader, let me advise thee, next to the Bible, let it be thy chief care, as thou art curious and careful for wholesome food, for the health and preservation of thy body, so be no less careful to make sound and solid divinity books thy chief study and delight.

Thomas Brooks.

Godliness is Great Gain.

"Godliness is great gain." O the joy, the peace, the comfort, the rest that saints meet with in the ways and service of God! They find that religious services are not empty things, but things in which God is pleased to discover his beauty and glory to their souls. "My soul thirsts for God," saith David, "that I might see thy beauty and thy glory, as I have seen Thee in thy sanctuary." O the sweet looks, the sweet words, the sweet hints, the sweet joggings, the sweet influences, the sweet love-letters that gracious souls have from heaven, when they wait upon God in holy and heavenly services, the least of which will darken and outweigh all the bravery and glory of this world, and richly recompense the soul for all the troubles, afflictions, and dangers that have attended it in the service of God! Oh! the saints can say, under all their troubles and afflictions, that they have meat to eat, and drink to drink, that the world knows not of; that they have such incomes, such refreshments, such warmings, etc., that they would not exchange for all the honours, riches, and dainties of this world! Ah! let but a Christian compare his external losses with his spiritual, internal, and external gain, and he shall find that, for every penny he loses in the service of God, he gains a pound; and for every pound that he loses, he gains a hundred; for every hundred lost, he gains a thousand. We lose pins in his service, and find pearls;

we lose the favour of the creature, and peace with the creature, and, haply, the comforts and contents of the creature, and we gain the favour of God, peace with conscience, and the comforts and contents of a better life. Ah, did the men of this world know the sweet that saints enjoy in afflictions, they would rather choose Manasseh's iron chain than his golden crown; they would rather be Paul a prisoner, than Paul rapt up in the third heaven! For "light afflictions," they shall have "a weight of glory;" for a few afflictions, they shall have these joys, pleasures, and contents, that are as the stars of heaven, or as the sands of the sea that cannot be numbered; for momentary afflictions, they shall have an eternal crown of glory.

VALUE OF THE TRUTH.

Solomon bids us buy the truth, but doth not tell us what it must cost, because we must get it though it be ever so dear. We must love it both shining and scorching. Every parcel of truth is precious, as the filings of gold; we must either live with it or die for it. As Ruth said to Naomi, "Whither thou goest I will go, and where thou lodgest I will lodge, and nothing but death shall part thee and me:" so must gracious spirits say, Where truth goes I will go, and where truth lodges I will lodge, and nothing but death shall part me and the truth. A man may lawfully sell his house, land, and jewels; but truth is a jewel that exceeds all price, and must not be sold: it is our heritage. "Thy testimonies have I taken as an heritage forever." It is a legacy that our forefathers have bought with their blood, which should make us willing to lay down anything, and to lay out anything, that we may, with the wise merchant in the Gospel, purchase this precious pearl, which is more worth than heaven and earth, and which will make a man live happily, die comfortably, and reign eternally.

THE HAPPIEST MAN.

It is not the knowing, nor the talking, nor the reading man, but the *doing* man that at last will be found the happiest man.

SATAN'S WILES.

Satan with ease puts fallacies upon us by his golden baits, and then he leads us and leaves us in a fool's paradise. He promises the soul honour, pleasure, profit, etc., but pays the soul with the greatest contempt, shame, and loss that can be.

ACTION A CHRISTIAN DUTY.

If it be not strong upon thy heart to practice what thou readest, to what end dost thou read? To increase thine own condemnation? If thy light and knowledge be not turned into practice, the more knowing man thou art, the more miserable man wilt thou be in the day of recompense; thy light and knowledge will more torment thee than all the devils in hell; thy knowledge will be that rod that will eternally lash thee, and that scorpion that will forever bite thee, and that worm that will everlastingly gnaw thee; therefore, read and labour to know, that thou mayest do, or else thou art undone forever. When Demosthenes was asked, What was the first part of an orator, what the second, and what the third? he answered, Action. The same may I say. If any should ask me, What is the first, the second, the third part of a Christian? I must answer, Action; as that man who reads that he may know, and who labours that he may do, will have two heavens—a heaven of joy, peace, and comfort on earth, and a heaven of glory and happiness after death

THE DANGER OF RICHES.

Adversity hath slain her thousand, but prosperity her ten thousand.

BITTER SWEETS.

Many long to be meddling with the murdering morsels of sin, which nourish not, but rent and consume the belly, the soul that receives them. Many eat that on earth that they may digest in hell. Sin's murdering morsels will deceive those that devour them. Adam's apple was a bitter sweet; Esau's mess was a bitter sweet; the Israelite's quails a bitter sweet; Jonathan's honey a bitter sweet; and Adonijah's dainties a bitter sweet. After the meal is ended, then comes the reckoning. Men must not think to dine and dance with the devil, and then to sup with Abraham, Isaac, and Jacob in the kingdom of heaven; to feed upon the poison of asps, and yet that the viper's tongue should not slay them.

When the asp stings a man, it doth first tickle in so as it makes him laugh, till the poison, by little and little, gets to the heart, and then it pains him more than ever it delighted him. So doth sin; it may please a little at first, but it will pain the soul with a witness at last; yea, if there were the least real delight in sin, there could be no perfect hell, where men shall be most perfectly tormented with their sin.

The Power of Sin.

Sin gives Satan a power over us, and an advantage to accuse us, and to lay claim to us, as those that wear his badge. It is of a very bewitching nature; it bewitches the soul, where it is upon the throne, that the soul cannot leave it, though it perish eternally by it. Sin so bewitches the soul, that it makes the soul call evil good, and good evil; bitter sweet, and sweet bitter, light darkness, and darkness light; and a soul thus bewitched with sin will stand it out to the death, at the sword's point with God; let God strike and wound, and cut to the very bone, yet the bewitched soul cares not, fears not, but will still hold on in a course of wickedness, as you may see in Pharaoh, Baalam, and Judas. Tell the bewitched soul that sin is a viper that will certainly kill when it is not killed, that sin often kills secretly, insensibly, eternally, yet the bewitched soul cannot, nor will not, cease from sin.

A Good Christian.

Two things make a good Christian—good actions and good aims; and though a good aim doth not make a bad action good, as in Uriah, yet a bad aim makes a good action bad, as in Jehu, whose justice was approved, but his policy punished.

SMALL SINS.

The viper is killed by the little ones that are nourished and cherished in her belly: so are many men eternally killed and betrayed by the little sins, as they call them, that are nourished in their own bosoms. Caesar was stabbed with bodkins. Pope Adrian was choked with a gnat. A scorpion is little, yet able to sting a lion to death. A mouse is but little, yet killeth an elephant, if he gets up into his trunk. The leopard being great, is poisoned with a head of garlic. The smallest errors prove many times most dangerous. It is as much treason to coin pence as bigger pieces.

BEWARE OF SIN.

A poisonous pill is never a whit the less poisonous because it is gilded over with gold; nor a wolf is never a whit the less a wolf because he hath put on a sheep's skin; nor the devil is never a whit less a devil because he appears sometimes like an angel of light. So neither is sin any whit the less filthy and abominable by its being painted over with virtue's colours.

MEDITATION.

It is not hasty reading, but serious meditating upon holy and heavenly truths, that makes them prove sweet and profitable to the soul. It is not the bee's touching of the flower that gathers honey, but her abiding for a time upon a flower that draws out the sweet. It is not he that reads most, but he that meditates most, that will prove the choicest, sweetest, wisest, and strongest Christian.

Satan's Duplicity.

Till we have sinned, Satan is a parasite: when we have sinned, he is a tyrant.

Spiritual Pride.

Oh, take heed of spiritual pride! Pride fills our fancies, and weakens our graces, and makes room in our hearts for error. There are no men on earth so soon entangled, and so easily conquered by error, as proud souls. Oh, it is dangerous to love to be wise above what is written, to be curious and unsober in your desire of knowledge, and to trust to your own capacities and abilities to undertake to pry into all secrets, and to be puffed up with a carnal mind! Souls that are thus a-soaring up above the bounds and limits of humility, usually fall into the very worst of errors, as experience doth daily evidence.

True Goodness.

It is in fashion to seem at least to be good among the good; but to be really good among those that are bad, that are eminently bad, argues not only a truth of goodness, but a great degree of goodness.

A Pertinent Question.

A company of near friends dining together one Sabbath-day, one that was at table, to prevent impertinent discourse, said "that it was a question whether they should all go to heaven or no," which struck them all into a dump, and caused every one to enter into a serious consideration with themselves. One thought, if any of this company go to hell, it must be I; and so thought another and another; and indeed so thought every one then present, — as well servants that waited as those that sat at table, as it was afterwards acknowledged; and, through the mercy and blessing of God, this speech so wrought upon the spirits of most of them, that it proved the first instrumental means of their conversion.

OPPORTUNITY.

The ancients painted opportunity with a hairy fore-head, but bald behind, to signify that, while a man hath opportunity before him, he may lay hold on it; but if he suffer it to slip away, he cannot pull it back again.

HOLD FAST THE TRUTH.

As men take no hold on the arm of flesh till they let go the arm of God, so men take no hold of error till they let go their hold of truth; therefore hold fast the truth. Truth is thy crown; hold fast thy crown, and let no man take thy crown from thee. Hath not God made truth sweet to thy soul, yea, sweeter than honey, or the honeycomb? and wilt not thou go on to heaven, feeding upon truth, that heavenly honeycomb, as Samson did of his honeycomb? Ah, souls, have you not found truth sweetening your spirits, and raising your spirits, and corroborating your spirits? Have you not found truth a guide to lead you, a staff to uphold you, a cordial to strengthen you, and a plaster to heal you? And will not you hold fast the truth? Hath not truth been your best friend in your worst days? Hath not truth stood by you when friends have forsaken you? Hath not truth done more for you than all the world could do against you, and will you not hold fast the truth? Is not truth your right eye, without which you cannot see for Christ? And your right hand, with which you cannot do for Christ? And your right foot, without which you cannot walk with Christ? And will not you hold fast truth? Oh! hold fast the truth in your judgments and understandings, in your wills and affections, in your profession and conversation!

Truth is more precious than gold or rubies, and all the things thou canst desire are not to be compared to her. Truth is that heavenly glass wherein we may see the lustre and glory of Divine wisdom, power, greatness, love, and mercifulness. In this glass you may see the face of Christ, the favour of Christ, the riches of Christ, and the heart of Christ, beating and working sweetly towards your souls. Oh! let your souls cleave to the truth, as Ruth did to Naomi, and say, "I will not leave truth, nor return from following after truth; but where truth goes I will go, and where truth lodges I will lodge; and nothing but death will part truth and my soul." What John said to the Church at Philadelphia, I may say to you: "Hold fast that which thou hast, that no man take thy crown." The crown is the top of royalties: such a thing is truth; let no man take thy crown. "Hold fast the faithful word," as Titus speaks. You had better let go anything than truth; you had better let go your honours and riches, your friends and pleasures, and the world's favours; yea, your nearest and dearest relations, ay, your very lives, than to let go truth. Oh, keep the truth, and that will make you safe and happy forever. Blessed are those souls that are kept by truth!

WHY MEN LOVE THE WORLD.

The main reason why men doat upon the world, and damn their souls to get the world, is because they are not acquainted with a greater glory. Men ate acorns, till they were acquainted with the use of wheat. Ah, were men more acquainted with what union and communion with God means, what it is to have "a new name, and a new stone, that none knows but he that hath it;" did they but taste more of heaven, and live more in heaven, and had more glorious hopes of going to heaven, ah, how easily would they have the moon under their feet!

THE BREVITY OF LIFE.

Our life is but as a few days. It is but as a vapour, a span, a flower, a shadow, a dream; and therefore Seneca saith well, that "though death be before the old man's face, yet he may be as near the young man's back." Man's life is the shadow of smoke, the dream of a shadow. One doubteth whether to call it a dying life, or a living death.

REMEMBER THY CREATOR.

"Remember now thy Creator in the days of thy youth, while the evil days come not, nor the years draw nigh, when thou shalt say, I have no pleasure in them!" Remember now; I say now! Now is an atom, it will puzzle the wisdom of a philosopher, the skill of an angel, to divide. Now is a monosyllable in all learned languages: "Remember *now* thy Creator!" Remember Him presently, instantly, for thou dost not know what a day, what an hour, may bring forth; thou canst not tell what deadly sin, what deadly temptation, what deadly judgment, may overtake thee, if thou dost not now, even now, "remember thy Creator."

THE UNCERTAINTY OF DEATH.

Death may suddenly and unexpectedly seize upon you; you have no lease of your lives. Youth is as fickle as old age. The young man may find graves enough of his length in burial-places. As green wood and old logs meet in one fire, so young sinners and old sinners meet in one hell and burn together. When the young man is in his spring and prime, then he is cut off and dies: "One dieth in his full strength, being wholly at ease and quiet; his breasts are full of milk, and his bones are moistened with marrow." David's children die when young, so did Job's and Jeroboam's. Every day's experience tells us, that the young man's life is as much a vapour as the old man's is.

NOW IS THE TIME.

He that will not at the first-hand buy good counsel cheap, shall at the second-hand buy repentance over dear.

MAKE SURE OF ETERNITY.

Ah! young men and women, God calls, and the blood of Jesus Christ calls, and the Spirit of Christ in the Gospel calls, and the rage of Satan calls, and your sad state and condition call, and the happiness and blessedness of glorified saints call,—these all call aloud upon you to make sure a glorious eternity, before you fall out into that dreadful ocean. All your eternal good depends upon the short and uncertain moments of your lives; and if the thread of your lives should be out before a happy eternity is made sure, woe to you that ever you were born! Do not say, O young man, that thou art young, and hereafter will be time enough to provide for eternity; for eternity may be at the door, ready to carry thee away forever. Every day's experience speaks out eternity to be as near the young man's back as it is before the old man's face. O grasp today the diadem of a blessed eternity, lest thou art cut off before the morning comes! Though there is but one way to come into this world, yet there are a thousand thousand ways to be sent out of it.

INSINUATING POWER OF SIN.

Sin is of an encroaching nature; it creeps on the soul by degrees, step by step, till it hath the soul to the very height of sin. David gives way to his wandering eye, and this led him to those foul sins that caused God to break his bones, and to turn his day into night, and to leave his soul in great darkness. Jacob and Peter, and other saints, have found this true by woeful experience, that the yielding to a lesser sin hath been the ushering in of a greater. The little thief will open the door, and make way for the greater; and the little wedge knocked in will make way for the greater. Satan will first draw thee to sit with the drunkard, and then to sip with the drunkard, and then at last to be drunk with the drunkard. He will draw thee to be unclean in thy thoughts, and then to be unclean in thy looks, and then to be unclean in thy words, and at last to be unclean in thy practices. He will first draw thee to look upon the golden wedge, and then to handle the golden wedge, and then at last, by wicked ways, to gain the golden wedge, though thou runnest the hazard of losing God and thy soul forever; as you may see in Gehazi, Achan, and Judas, and many in these our days.

The Uses of Affliction.

Afflictions are God's furnace, by which He cleanses his people from their dross. Affliction is a fire to purge out our dross, and to make virtue shine; it is a potion to carry away ill humours, better than all the *benedictum medicamentum*, as physicians call them. Aloes kill worms; colds and frosts do destroy vermin; so do afflictions the corruptions that are in our hearts.

Earnest Prayer.

"The working prayer of a righteous man availeth much." That prayer that sets the whole man a-work, will work wonders in heaven, in the heart, and in the earth. Earnest prayer, like Saul's sword and Jonathan's bow, never returns empty.

God's Justice.

God is as just as He is merciful. As the Scriptures speak Him out to be a very merciful God, so they speak Him out to be a very just God. Witness his casting the angels out of heaven, and his binding them in chains of darkness till the judgment of the great day; and witness his turning Adam out of Paradise, his drowning of the old world, and his raining hell out of heaven upon Sodom; and witness all the crosses, losses, sicknesses, and diseases that be in the world; and witness Tophet, that was prepared of old; witness his "treasuring up of wrath against the day of wrath, unto the revelation of the just judgments of God;" but, above all, witness the pouring forth of all his wrath upon his bosom Son, when He did bear the sins of his people, and cried out, "My God, my God, why hast thou forsaken me!"

EVIL FOR GOOD.

To render good for evil is Divine, to render good for good is human, to render evil for evil is brutish; but to render evil for good is devilish; and from this evil deliver my soul, O God.

GOD'S FORBEARANCE NO QUITTANCE.

God's forbearance is no quittance. The day is at hand when He will pay wicked men for the abuse of old and new mercies. If He seem to be slow, yet He is sure. He hath leaden heels, but iron hands. The farther He stretcheth his bow, or draweth his arrow, the deeper He will wound in the day of vengeance. Men's actions are all in print in heaven, and God will, in the day of account, read them aloud in the ears of all the world, that they may all say Amen to that righteous sentence that He shall pass upon all despisers and abusers of mercy.

THE CURSE OF GOD.

The curse of God haunts the wicked, as it were a fury, in all his ways. In the city it attends him, in the country hovers over him; coming in, it accompanies him; going forth, it follows him; and in travel it is his comrade. It fills his store with strife, and mingles the wrath of God with his sweetest morsels. It is a moth in his wardrobe, murrain among his cattle, mildew in the field, rot among sheep, and ofttimes makes the fruit of his loins his greatest vexation and confusion. There is no solid joy, nor lasting peace, nor pure comfort, that attends sinners in their sinful ways. There is a sword of vengeance that doth every moment hang over their heads by a small thread; and what joy and content can attend such souls, if the eye of conscience be but so far open as to see the sword? Ah! the horrors and terrors, the tremblings and shakings, that attend their souls!

A Believer's Inheritance.

A believer's inheritance, his glory, his happiness, his blessedness, shall be as fresh and flourishing after he hath been many thousand thousands of years in heaven as it was at his first entrance into it. Earthly inheritances are like tennis-balls, which are bandied up and down from one to another, and in time wore out. The creature is all shadow and vanity; it is *filia noctis*, like Jonah's gourd. Man can sit under its shadow but a little, little while; it soon decays and dies; it quickly fades and withers. There is a worm at the root of all earthly inheritances, that will consume them in time. All earthly comforts and contents are but like a fair picture that is drawn upon the ice, which continueth not; or like the morning cloud, that soon passeth away; but a believer's inheritance endureth forever. When this world shall be no more, when time shall be no more, the inheritance of the saints shall be fresh, flourishing, and continuing. With Augustine, we will say: "What will that life be, or rather what will not that life be, since all good either is not at all, or is in such a life? Light, which place cannot comprehend; voices and music, which time cannot ravish away; odours, which are never dissipated; a feast, which is never consumed; a blessing, which eternity bestoweth, but eternity shall never see at an end. So this, all this, is the heritage of all God's Jacobs."

THE EVIL OF PROSPERITY.

Prosperity hath been a stumbling-block, at which millions have stumbled and fallen, and broke the neck of their souls forever.

CHRISTIAN SINCERITY.

Sincerity is the shine, the lustre, the beauty, the glory of all a Christian's graces. A sincere soul is like a crystal glass with a light in the midst of it, which gives light every way. A sincere soul is like the violet, which grows low, and hides itself and its own sweetness, as much as may be, with its own leaves.

A CHRISTIAN'S HOPE.

A Christian's hope is not like that of Pandora, which may fly out of the box, and bid the soul farewell. No, it is like the morning light; the least beam of it shall commence into a complete sunshine; it is *aurora gaudii,* and it shall shine forth brighter and brighter till perfect day.

Life in Heaven.

In heaven there shall be no sin, no devil, no sinner, no false friends; there shall be nothing, there shall not be the least thing that may interrupt a saint's rest. Heaven is above all winds and weather, storms and tempests, earthquakes and heartquakes. There is only that which is amiable and desirable; there is nothing to cloud a Christian's joy, or to interrupt a Christian's rest. When once a soul is asleep in the bosom of Abraham, none can awake him, none can molest or disturb him. Here is joy without sorrow, blessedness without misery, health without sickness, light without darkness, abundance without want, beauty without deformity, honour without disgrace, ease without labour, and peace without interruption or perturbation. Here shall be eyes without tears, hearts without fears, and souls without sin. Here shall be no evil to molest the soul; here shall be all good to cheer the soul, and all happiness to satisfy the soul; and what then can possibly interrupt the rest of the soul?

The Power of Error.

Gross errors make the heart foolish, and render the life loose, and the soul light in the eyes of God. Error spreads and frets like a gangrene, and renders the soul a leper in the sight of God.

Affection.

Luther fitly calls affliction "The Christian man's divinity."

THE TRIALS OF LIFE.

This life is full of trials, full of troubles, and full of changes. Sin within, and Satan and the world without, will keep a Christian from rest, till he comes to rest in the bosom of Christ. The life of a Christian is a race; but what rest have they that are still a-running their race? The life of a Christian is a warfare; and what rest have they that are engaged in a constant warfare? The life of a Christian is the life of a pilgrim; and what rest hath a pilgrim, who is still a-travelling from place to place? A pilgrim is like Noah's dove, that could find no rest for the sole of her foot. The fears, the snares, the cares, the changes, etc., that attend believers in this world, are such that will keep them from taking up their rest here. A Christian hears these words always sounding in his ears, "Arise, for this is not thy resting-place." A man may as well expect to find heaven in hell, as expect to find rest in this world. What misery do we not undergo in this life? What storms and tempests do we not endure? With what troubles are we not tossed? Whose worth is spared? Man's sorrows begin when his days begin, and his sorrows are multiplied as his days are multiplied; his whole life is but one continued grief. Labour wears him, care tears him, fears toss him, losses vex him, dangers trouble him, crosses disquiet him, nothing pleases him; in the day he wishes, Would God it were night, and in the night, Would God it were day; before he rises he sighs; before he washes he weeps; before he feeds he fears; under all his abundance he is in wants; and "in the midst of his sufficiency he is in straits."

GOD AND SIN.

God is light, sin is darkness; God is life, sin is death; God is heaven, sin is hell; God is beauty, sin is deformity.

GOD OPPOSED TO ALL SIN.

Those sins which we are apt to account small, have brought upon men the greatest wrath of God, as the eating of an apple, gathering a few sticks on the Sabbath-day, and touching of the ark. Oh! the dreadful wrath that these sins brought down upon the heads and hearts of men! The least sin is contrary to the law of God, the nature of God, the being of God, and the glory of God; and therefore it is often punished severely by God. And do not we see daily the vengeance of the Almighty falling upon the bodies, names, states, families, and souls of men, for those sins that are but little ones in their eyes? Surely, if we are not utterly left of God, and blinded by Satan, we cannot but see it. Oh! therefore, when Satan says it is but a little one, do thou say, Oh! but those sins that thou callest little are such as will cause God to rain hell out of heaven upon sinners, as he did upon the Sodomites.

THE BEGINNING OF SIN.

Corruption in the heart, when it breaks forth, is like a breach in the sea, which begins in a narrow passage, till it eats through and casts all before it. The debates of the soul are quick, and soon ended, and that may be done in a moment that may undo a man forever. When a man hath begun to sin, he knows not where, or when, or how he shall make a stop of sin. Usually the soul goes on from evil to evil, from folly to folly, till it be ripe for eternal misery. Men usually grow from being naught to be very naught, and from being very naught to be stark naught; and then God sets them at naught forever.

SIN'S MISCHIEVOUSNESS.

It cast angels out of heaven, and Adam out of Paradise; it laid the first corner-stone in hell, and brought in all the curses, crosses, and miseries that be in the world; and it makes men liable to all temporal, spiritual, and eternal wrath; it hath made men Godless, Christless, hopeless, and heavenless.

THE VIRTUE OF DIVINE LOVE.

As there is an attractive, so there is a compulsive virtue in Divine love. Love to Christ and souls will make a man willing to spend and be spent. He that prays himself to death, that preaches himself to death, that studies himself to death, that sweats himself to death, for the honour of Christ and the good of souls, shall be no loser in the end. Divine love is like a rod of myrtle, which, as Pliny reports, makes the traveller that carries it in his hand that he shall never be faint and weary. Divine love is very operative; *si non operatur, non est;* if it do not work, it is an argument it is not at all. Divine love, like fire, is not idle, but active. He that loves cannot be barren. Love will make the soul constant and abundant in well-doing. God admits none to heaven, saith Justin Martyr, but such as can persuade Him by their works that they love Him. The very heathen Seneca hath observed, that God doth not love his children with a weak, womanish affection, but with a strong, masculine love; and, certainly, they that love the Lord strongly,—that love Him with a masculine love,—they cannot but lay out their little all for Him and his glory.

GOD'S GREATNESS.

God hath in himself all the good of angels, of men, and universal nature; He hath all glories, all dignities, all riches, all treasures, all pleasures, all comforts, all delights, all joys, all beatitudes, God is that one infinite perfection in himself which is eminently and virtually all perfections of the creatures, and, therefore, He is firstly to be sought. Abstracts do better express Him than concretes and adjectives. He is being, bonity, power, wisdom, justice, mercy, goodness, and love itself, and therefore worthy to be sought before all other things.

DEATH THE GAIN OF THE CHRISTIAN.

A Christian's dying day is the Lord's pay-day; that is, a time to receive wages, not to do work.

THE UNCERTAINTY OF LIFE.

As the life of man is very short, so it is very uncertain. Now well, now sick; alive this hour, and dead the next. Death doth not always give warning beforehand. Sometimes he gives the mortal blow suddenly; he comes behind with his dart, and strikes a man at the heart before he saith, "Have I found thee, O mine enemy?" Eutychus fell down dead suddenly; death suddenly arrested David's sons and Job's sons; Augustus died in a compliment, Galba with a sentence, Vespasian with a jest; Zeuxis died laughing at the picture of an old woman, which he drew with his own hands; Sophocles was choked with the stone in a grape; Diodorus, the logician, died for shame that he could not answer a jocularly-put question propounded at the table by Stilpo; Joannes Measius, preaching upon the raising of the woman of Nain's son from the dead, within three hours after died himself .

Ah, young men and women, have you not cause, great cause, to be good betimes? for death is sudden in his approaches. Nothing more sure than death, and nothing more uncertain than life. Therefore, know the Lord betimes, turn from your sins betimes; lay hold on the Lord, and make peace with Him betimes, that you may never say, as Caesar Borgia said when he was sick to death: "When I lived," he said, "I provided for everything but death; now I must die, and am unprovided to die!"

THE CHRISTIAN'S SAFETY.

A believer's treasure is always safe in the hands of Christ. His life is safe, his soul is safe, his grace is safe, his comfort is safe, and his crown is safe in the hands of Christ. "I know Him in whom I have believed, and that He is able to keep that which I have committed unto Him until that day," saith the apostle. The child's most precious things are most scarce in his father's hands; so are our souls, our graces, and our comforts in the hands of Christ.

Wʜʏ Gᴏᴅ Sᴇɴᴅѕ Aғғʟɪᴄᴛɪᴏɴ.

"He afflicts us for our profit, that we might be partakers of his holiness." The flowers smell sweetest after a shower; vines bear the better for bleeding; the walnut-tree is most fruitful when most beaten. Saints spring and thrive most internally when they are most externally afflicted. Afflictions are called by some "the mother of virtue." Manasseh's chain was more profitable to him than his crown. Luther could not understand some Scriptures till he was in affliction. The Christ-cross is no letter, and yet that taught him more than all the letters in the row. God's house of correction is his school of instruction. All the stones that came about Stephen's ears did but knock him closer to Christ, the corner-stone. The waves did but lift Noah's ark nearer to heaven; and the higher the waters grew, the more near the ark was lifted up to heaven. Afflictions do lift up the soul to more rich, clear, and full enjoyments of God.

Gᴏᴅ'ѕ Gᴇᴍѕ ᴀɴᴅ Jᴇᴡᴇʟѕ.

When Munster lay sick, and his friends asked him how he did and how he felt himself, he pointed to his sores and ulcers, whereof he was full, and said, "These are God's gems and jewels, wherewith He decketh his best friends, and to me they are more precious than all the gold and silver in the world." A soul at first conversion is but rough cast; but God by afflictions doth square and fit and fashion it for that glory above, which doth speak them out to flow from precious love; therefore the afflictions that do attend the people of God should be no bar to holiness, nor no motive to draw the soul to ways of wickedness.

THE SANCTIFYING INFLUENCE OF AFFLICTION.

When Tiribazus, a noble Persian, was arrested, he drew out his sword, and defended himself; but when they told him that they came to carry him to the king, he willingly yielded. So, though a saint may at first stand a little out, yet when he remembers that afflictions are to carry nearer to God, he yields, and kisses the rod. Afflictions are like the prick at the nightingale's breast, that awakes her and puts her upon her sweet and delightful singing.

Afflictions they serve to revive and recover decayed graces; they inflame that love that is cold, and they quicken that faith that is decaying, and they put life into those hopes that are withering, and spirits into those joys and comforts that are languishing. Musk, saith one, when it hath lost its sweetness, if it be put into the sink amongst filth, it recovers it. So do afflictions recover and revive decayed graces. The more saints are beaten with the hammer of afflictions, the more they are made the trumpets of God's praises, and the more are their graces revived and quickened. Adversity abases the loveliness of the world that might entice us; it abates the lustiness of the flesh within, that might incite us to folly and vanity; and it abets the spirit in his quarrel to the two former, which tends much to the reviving and recovering of decayed graces.

THE PRECIOUS FOUNTAIN.

I have read of a fountain that at noonday is cold, and at midnight it grows warm. So many a precious soul is cold God-wards, and heaven-wards, and holiness-wards, in the day of prosperity, that grow warm God-wards, and heaven-wards, and holiness-wards, in the midnight of adversity.

THE HEATHEN AND HIS SOUL.

It was the speech of an heathen, when as by the tyrant he was commanded to be put into a mortar, and to be beaten to pieces with an iron pestle, he cries out to his persecutors, "You do but beat the vessel, the case, the husk of Anaxarchus; you do not beat me." His body was to him but as a case, a husk; he counted his soul himself, which they could not reach.

THE EVIL OF PROSPERITY.

I have read of one who, when anything fell out prosperously, would read over the Lamentation of Jeremiah, and that kept his heart tender, humbled, and low. Prosperity doth not contribute more to the puffing up the soul, than adversity doth to the bowing down of the soul. This the saints by experience find; and therefore they can kiss and embrace the Cross, as others do the world's crown.

THE USE OF AFFLICTION.

It was a speech of a German divine in his sickness, "In this disease I have learned how great God is, and what the evil of sin is; I never knew to purpose what God was before, nor what sin meant, till now." Afflictions are a crystal glass, wherein the soul hath the clearest sight of the ugly face of sin. In this glass the soul comes to see sin to be but a bitter-sweet; yea, in this glass the soul comes to see sin not only to be an evil, but to be the greatest evil in the world, to be an evil far worse than hell itself.

THE CRUELTY OF SIN.

THE Rabbins, to scare their scholars from sin, were wont to tell them, "That sin made God's head ache;" and saints under the rod have found, by woeful experience, that sin makes not only their heads, but their hearts ache also.

AFFLICTION GOD'S TRIAL.

Afflictions are like pinching frosts, that will search us; where we are most unsound, we shall soonest complain, and where most corruptions lie, we shall most shrink. We try metal by knocking; if it sound well, then we like it. So God tries his by knocking, and if under knocks they yield a pleasant sound, God will turn their night into day, and their bitter into sweet, and their cross into a crown; and they shall hear that voice, "Arise, and shine; for the glory of the Lord is risen upon thee, and the favours of the Lord are flowing in on thee."

THE WICKED SHALL PERISH.

There is not a wicked man in the world that is set up with Lucifer, as high as heaven, but shall with Lucifer be brought down as low as hell.

Denying God.

Austin, writing upon John, tells a story of a certain man, that was of an opinion that the devil did make the fly, and not God. Saith one to him, If the devil made flies, then the devil made worms, and God did not make them, for they are living creatures as well as flies. True, said he, the devil did make worms. But, said the other, if the devil did make worms, then he made birds, beasts, and man. He granted all. Thus, saith Austin, by denying God in the fly, became to deny God in man, and to deny the whole creation.

Hypocrisy.

There is not a greater nor a clearer argument to prove a man a hypocrite, than to be quick-sighted abroad and blind at home; than to see "a mote in another man's eye, and not a beam in his own eye;" than to use spectacles to behold other men's sins rather than looking-glasses to behold his own; rather to be always holding his finger upon other men's sores, and to be amplifying and aggravating other men's sins, than mitigating his own.

Great and Small Sins.

I know not, saith one, whether the maintenance of the least sin be not worse than the commission of the greatest: for this may be of frailty, that argues obstinacy. A little hole in the ship sinks it; a small breach in a sea-bank carries away all before it; a little stab at the heart kills a man; and a little sin, without a great deal of mercy, will damn a man.

SUFFERING FOR GOD.

I have read of that noble servant of God, Marcus Arethusius, minister of a church in the time of Constantine, who in Constantine's time had been the case of overthrowing an idol's temple; afterwards, when Julian came to be emperor, he would force the people of that place to build it up again. They were ready to do it, but he refused; whereupon those that were his own people, to whom he preached, took him, and stripped him of all his clothes, and abused his naked body, and gave it up to the children, to lance it with their penknives, and then caused him to be put in a basket, and anointed his naked body with honey, and set him in the sun, to be stung with wasps. And all this cruelty they showed, because he would not do anything towards the building up of this idol temple; nay, they came to this, that if he would do but the least towards it, if he would give but a halfpenny to it, they would save him. But he refused all, though the giving of a halfpenny might have saved his life; and in doing this, he did but live up to that principle that most Christians talk of, and all profess, but few come up to, viz., that we must choose rather to suffer the worst of torments that men and devils can invent and inflict, than to commit the least sin, whereby God should be dishonoured, our consciences wounded, religion reproached, and our own souls endangered.

THE PENITENT THIEF.

Mr. Perkins mentions a good man, but very poor, who, being ready to starve, stole a lamb, and being about to eat it with his poor children, and as his manner was afore meat, to crave a blessing, durst not do it, but fell into a great perplexity of conscience, and acknowledged his fault to the owner, promising payment if ever he should be able.

God's Mercy.

When mercy is despised, then justice takes the throne. God is like a prince, that sends not his army against rebels before He hath sent his pardon, and proclaimed it by a herald of arms: He first hangs out the white flag of mercy; if this wins men in, they are happy forever; but if they stand out, then God will put forth his red flag of justice and judgment; if the one is despised, the other shall be felt with a witness.

The Devil's Logic.

There is nothing in the world that renders a man more unlike to a saint, and more like to Satan, than to argue from mercy to sinful liberty; from Divine goodness to licentiousness. This is the devil's logic, and in whomsoever you find it, you may write, "This soul is lost." A man may as truly say, the sea burns, or fire cools, as that free grace and mercy should make a soul truly gracious to do wickedly.

Temptation and Sin.

It is the greatest folly to adventure the going to hell for a small matter. "I tasted but a little honey," said Jonathan, "and I must die." It is a most unkind and unfaithful thing to break with God for a little. Little sins carry with them but little temptations to sin, and then a man shows most viciousness and unkindness when he sins on a little temptation. It is devilish to sin without a temptation; it is little less than devilish to sin on a little occasion. The less the temptation is to sin, the greater is that sin. Saul's sin in not staying for Samuel, was not so much in the matter, but it was much in the malice of it; for though Samuel had not come at all, yet Saul should not have offered sacrifice; but this cost him dear, his soul and kingdom.

TURN FROM SIN.

He that turns not from every sin, turns not aright from any one sin. Every sin strikes at the honour of God, the being of God, the glory of God, the heart of Christ, the joy of the Spirit, and the peace of a man's conscience; and therefore a soul truly penitent strikes at all, hates all, conflicts with all, and will labour to draw strength from a crucified Christ to crucify all. A true penitent knows neither father nor mother, neither right eye nor right hand, but will pluck out the one and cut off the other. Saul spared but one Agag, and that cost him his soul and his kingdom. Besides, repentance is not only a turning from all sin, but also a turning to all good; to a love of all good, to a prizing of all good, and to a following after all good.

REPENTANCE A GIFT OF GOD.

Thou art as well able to melt adamant, as to melt thine own heart; to turn a flint into flesh, as to turn thine own heart to the Lord; to raise the dead and to make a world, as to repent. Repentance is a flower that grows not in nature's garden. "Can the Ethiopian change his skin, or the leopard his spots? then may ye also do good, that are accustomed to do evil." Repentance is a gift that comes down from above.

BE PREPARED FOR DEATH.

A Jewish Rabbi, pressing the practice of repentance upon his disciples, exhorting them to be sure to repent the day before they died, one of them replied, that the day of any man's death was very uncertain. "Repent, therefore, every day," said the Rabbi, "and then you shall be sure to repent the day before you die."

TRUE REPENTANCE.

True repentance is a continued spring, where the waters of godly sorrow are always flowing.

THE GOLDEN CALF.

The Jews have a proverb, "That there is no punishment comes upon Israel in which there is not one ounce of the golden calf;" meaning that that was so great a sin, as that in every plague God remembered it; that it had an influence into every trouble that befell them.

THE PUNISHMENT OF THE WICKED.

Though God will not utterly take from them his loving-kindness, nor suffer his faithfulness to fail, nor break his covenant, nor alter the thing that is gone out of his mouth, yet will He "visit their transgression with a rod, and their iniquity with stripes." The Scripture abounds with instances of this kind. This is so known a truth among all that know anything of truth, that to cite more Scriptures to prove it would be to light a candle to see the sun at noon.

THE NEEDS OF WICKED MEN.

Wicked men are the most needy men in the world, yea, they want those two things that should render their mercies sweet, *viz.*, the blessing of God, and content with their condition, and without which their heaven is but hell on this side hell.

LOVING HURTFUL THINGS.

It was a good speech of an emperor: "You," said he, "gaze on my purple robe and golden crown, but did you know what cares are under it, you would not take it up from the ground to have it." It was a true saying of Augustine: "Many are miserable by loving hurtful things, but they are more miserable by having them." It is not what men enjoy, but the principle from whence it comes, that makes men happy. Much of these outward things do usually cause great distraction, great vexation, and great condemnation at last, to the possessors of them. If God gives them in his wrath, and do not sanctify them in his love, they will at last be witnesses against a man, and millstones forever to sink a man in that day when God shall call men to an account, not for the use, but for the abuse of mercy.

IMPROVEMENT OF TIME.

How many young men are now in everlasting chains, who would give ten thousand worlds, had they so many in their hands to give, to enjoy but an opportunity to hear one sermon more, to make one prayer more, to keep one Sabbath more, but cannot. This is their hell, their torment; this is the scorpion that is still biting; this is the worm that is always gnawing. Woe, woe to us, that we have neglected and trifled away those golden opportunities that once we had to get our sins pardoned, our natures changed, our hearts bettered, our consciences purged, and our souls saved, etc. I have read of a king, who, having no issue to succeed him, espying one day a well-favoured youth, took him to court, and committed him to tutors to instruct him, providing by his will, that if he proved fit for government, he should be crowned king; if not, he should be bound in chains and made a galley-slave. Now, when he grew to years, the king's executors, perceiving that he had sadly neglected those means and opportunities whereby he might have been fit for state-government, called him before them, and declared the king's will and pleasure concerning him, which was accordingly performed, for they caused him to be fettered, and committed to the galleys. Now, what tongue can express how much he was affected and afflicted with his sad and miserable state, especially when he considered with himself, that now he is chained who might have walked at liberty; now he is a slave who might have been a king; now he is overruled by Turks who might once have ruled over Christians. The application is easy.

THE DAY OF ACCOUNT.

God keeps an exact account of every penny that is laid out upon Him and his, and that is laid out against Him and his; and this is the day of account men shall know and feel, though now they wink and will not understand.

BEZA.

Among many things that Beza, in his last will and testament, gave God thanks for, this was the first and chief, that He, at the age of sixteen years, had called him to the knowledge of the truth, and so prevented many sins and sorrows that otherwise would have overtaken him, and have made his life less happy and more miserable.

TIIE SWIFTNESS OF TIME.

I have read of a devout man who, when he heard a clock strike, he would say, Here is one hour more passed that I have to answer for. Ah! young men, as time is very precious, so it is very short. Time is very swift; it is suddenly gone. In the 9th of Job, and the 25th verse, "My days are swifter than a post, they flee away, they see no good."

TIIE VALUE OF TIME.

The ancients emblemed time with wings, as it were, not running, but flying. Time is like the sun, that never stands still, but is still a-running his race. The sun did once stand still, yea, went back, but so did never time. Time is still running and flying. It is a bubble, a shadow, a dream. Can you seriously consider of this, young men, and not begin to be good betimes? Surely you cannot. Sirs! if the whole earth whereupon we tread were turned into a lump of gold, it were not able to purchase one minute of time. O the regrettings of the damned for misspending precious time! Oh, what would they not give to be free, and to enjoy the means of grace one hour! Ah! with what attention, with what intention, with what trembling and melting of heart, with what hungering and thirsting, would they hear the Word! Time, saith Bernard, were a good commodity in hell, and the traffic of it most gainful, where for one day a man would give ten thousand worlds, if he had them. Young men, can you in good earnest believe this, and not begin to be good betimes?

Picture of Time.

The Egyptians drew the picture of time with three heads: the first of a greedy wolf, gaping, for time past, because it hath ravenously devoured the memory of so many things past recalling; the second of a crowned lion, roaring, for time present, because it hath the principality of all actions, for which it calls loud; the third of a deceitful dog, fawning, for time to come, because it feeds some men with many flattering hopes, to their eternal undoing.

Death Inevitable.

Man is so poor a piece, that he no sooner begins to live, but he begins to die; his whole life is but a lingering death. Death every hour lies at the door. This serjeant constantly attends all men, in all places, companies, changes, and conditions. Petrarch telleth of one who, being invited to dinner the next day, answered, *Ego a multus annis crastinum non habui,* I have not had a morrow for this many years. Many dangers, many deaths, every hour surround these lives of ours. Here, saith one, *accedimus*, we enter into the world; *succedimus*, we succeed one another in the world; *decedimus*, we depart all out of the world.

TWO GLORIOUS SIGHTS.

There are two glorious sights in the world: the one is, a young man walking in his uprightness; and the other is, an old man walking in ways of righteousness.

THE JOURNEY OF LIFE.

I have read of an Italian poet, who brings in a proper young man, rich and potent, discoursing with Death in the habit of a mower, with his scythe in his hand, cutting down the life of man, "For all flesh is grass." And wilt thou not spare any man's person? saith the young man. I spare none, saith Death. Man's life is but a day, a short day, a winter's day. Ofttimes the sun goes down upon a man before it be well up. Your day is short, your work is great, your journey long, and therefore you should rise early, and set forward towards heaven betimes, as that man doth that hath a long journey to go in a winter's day.

THE NEW BIRTH.

When Joshaphat asked Barlaam how old he was, he answered, "Five and forty years old;" to whom Joshaphat replied, "Thou seemest to be seventy." "True," saith he, "if you reckon ever since I was born; but I count not those years which were spent in vanity."

The Good Life.

Ah, sirs! you never begin to live till you begin to be good in good earnest. There is the life of vegetation, and that is the life of plants; secondly, there is the life of sense, and that is the life of beasts; thirdly, there is the life of reason, and that is the life of man; fourthly, there is the life of grace, and that is the life of saints; and this life you do not begin to live till you begin to be good. If "a living dog is better than a dead lion," as the wise man speaks, and if a fly is more excellent than the heavens, because the fly hath life, which the heavens have not, as the philosopher saith, what a sad, dead, poor nothing is that person that is a stranger to the life of grace and goodness, that is dead even whilst he is alive!

Sowing and Reaping.

It is sad to be sowing your seed when you should be reaping your harvest; it is best to gather in the summer of youth against the winter of old age.

The Best Gift.

I have read of one Myrogenes, who, when great gifts were sent unto him, he sent them all back again, saying, I only desire this one thing at your master's hand: to pray for me that I may be saved for eternity.

Trifle Not with God.

It is a very sad and dangerous thing to trifle and dally with God, his word, his offers, our own souls, and eternity. Therefore, let all young people labour to be good betimes, and not to let Him that is goodness itself alone till He bath made them good; till He hath given them those hopes of eternity that will both make them good and keep them good; that will make them happy, and keep them happy, and that forever. If all this will not do, then know that ere long those fears of eternity, of misery, that beget that monster Despair, which, like Medusa's head, astonisheth with its very aspect, and strangles hope, which is the breath of the soul, will certainly overtake you; as it is said, *Dum Spiro, Spero*, so it may be inverted, *Dum Spero Spiro;* other miseries may wound the spirit, but despair kills it dead. My prayer shall be, that none of you may ever experience this sad truth, but that you may all be good in good earnest, betimes, which will yield you two heavens,—a heaven on earth, and a heaven after death.

OPPOSE NOT THE TRUTH.

When men stand out against the truth, when truth would enter, and men bar the door of their souls against the truth, God in justice gives up such souls to be deluded and deceived by error, to their eternal undoing.

THE WEIGHT OF GLORY.

Glory is such a great, such an exceeding, such an excessive, such an eternal weight, that no mortal is able to bear it. We must have better and larger hearts, and we must have stronger and broader backs, before we shall be capable of bearing that excellent, exceeding, and excelling weight of glory that is reserved in heaven for us. Nay, glory is such a weight, that when the saints shall enter into it, if then the Lord should not put under his everlasting arms and bear them up by his almighty power, it were impossible that they should be able to bear it. In this our frail mortal state, we are not able to bear the appearance, the presence, the glory of one angel.

LOVE THE TRUTH.

As you love your souls, do not tempt God, do not provoke God, by your withstanding truth and outfacing truth, to give you up to believe a lie, that you may be damned. There are no men on earth so fenced against error as those are that receive the truth in the love of it. Such souls are not "easily tossed to and fro, and carried about with every wind of doctrine by the sleight of men and cunning craftiness, wherein they lie in wait to deceive."

HOW TO RECEIVE TRUTH.

It is not he that receives most of the truth into his head, but he that receives most of the truth affectionately into his heart, that shall enjoy the happiness of having his judgment sound and clear, when others shall be deluded and deceived by them, who make it their business to infect the judgments and to undo the souls of men.

THE VIRTUE OF TRUTH.

There was more wit than grace in his speech that counselled his friends, "Not to come too nigh unto truth, lest his teeth should be beaten out with its heels." Ah! souls, if truth dwell plenteously in you, you are happy; if not, you are unhappy under all your greatest felicity. "It is with truth," said Melancthon, "as it is with holy water; every one praised it, and thought it had some rare virtue in it; but offer to sprinkle them with it, and they will shut their eyes, and turn away their faces-from it."

THE INDWELLING OF TRUTH.

It is not the hearing of truth, nor the knowing of truth, nor the commending of truth, nor the talking of truth, but the indwelling of truth in your souls, that will keep your judgments chaste and sound in the midst of all those glittering errors that betray many souls into his hands, that can easily "transform himself into an angel of light," that he may draw others to lie in chains of darkness with him forever. Oh, let not the Word be a stranger, but make it your choicest familiar! Then will you be able to stand in the day wherein many shall fall on your right hand, and on your left, by the subtlety of those that shall say, "Lo, here is Christ, or lo, there is Christ."

PROPAGATION OF ERROR.

Error makes the owner to suffer loss. All the pains and labour that men take to defend and maintain their errors, to spread abroad and infect the world with their errors, shall bring no profit, nor no comfort to them in that day, wherein "every man's work shall be made manifest, and the fire shall try it of what sort it is," as the Apostle shows in that remarkable scripture. Ah! that all those that rise early and go to bed late, that spend their time, their strength, their spirits, their all, to advance and spread abroad God-dishonouring and soul-undoing opinions, would seriously consider of this, that they shall lose all the pains, cost, and charge that they have been, or shall be at, for the propagating of error; and if they are ever saved, it shall be by fire, as the Apostle there shows. Ah, sirs! Is it nothing to lay out your money for that which is not bread? and your strength for that which will not, which cannot, profit you in the day that you must make up your account, and all your works must be tried by fire? Ah! that such souls would now at last "buy the truth, and sell it not." Remember you can never over-buy it, whatsoever you give for it; you can never sufficiently sell it, if you should have all the world in exchange for it.

THE STUDY OF TRUTH.

One day, yea, one hour spent in the study of truth, or spreading abroad of truth, will yield the soul more comfort and profit, than many thousand years spent in the study and spreading abroad of corrupt and vain opinions, that have their rise from hell, and not from heaven; from the god of this world, and not from that God that shall at last judge this world, and all the corrupt opinions of men.

THE USES OF AFFLICTION.

The fourth remedy against this device of Satan is, to consider, *That God knows how to deliver from troubles by troubles, from afflictions by afflictions, from dangers by dangers.* God, by lesser troubles and afflictions, doth oftentimes deliver his people from greater, so that they shall say, We had perished, if we had not perished; we had been undone, if we had not been undone; we had been in danger, if we had not been in danger. God will so order the afflictions that befall you in the way of righteousness, that your souls shall say, We would not for all the world but that we had met with such and such troubles and afflictions; for surely, had not these befallen us, it would have been worse and worse with us. Oh! the carnal security, pride, formality, dead-heartedness, lukewarmness, censoriousness, and earthliness that God hath cured us of, by the trouble and dangers that we have met with in the ways and services of the Lord. I remember a story of a godly man, that as he was going to take shipping for France, he broke his leg; and it pleased Providence so to order it, that the ship that he should have gone in, at that very instant was cast away, and not a man saved; so by breaking a bone, his life was saved. So the Lord many times breaks our bones, but it is in order to the saving of our lives and our souls forever. He gives us a portion that makes us heartsick, but it is in order to the making us perfectly well, and to the purging of us from those ill humours that have made our heads ache, and God's heart ache, and our souls sick and heavy to the death, etc. Oh, therefore, let no danger or misery hinder thee from thy duty!

REASON WITH THY SOUL.

Reason thus with your souls: O, our souls, though such and such services be hard and difficult, yet are they not exceeding necessary for the honour of God, and the keeping up his name in the world, and the keeping under of sin, and the strengthening of weak graces, and so the reviving of languishing comforts, and for the keeping clear and bright your blessed evidences, and for the scattering of your fears, and for the raising of your hopes, and for the gladding the hearts of the righteous, and stopping the mouths of unrighteous souls, who are ready to take all advantages to blaspheme the name of God, and throw dirt and contempt upon his people and ways. Oh, never leave thinking on the necessity of this and that duty, till your souls be lifted up far above all the difficulties that do attend religious duties!

THE VANITY OF MAN.

Tell me, you that say all things under the sun are vanity,—if you do really believe what you say,—why do you spend more thoughts and time on the world than you do on Christ, heaven, and your immortal souls? Why do you, then, neglect your duty towards God, to get the world? Why do you, then, so eagerly pursue after the world, and are so cold in your pursuing after God, Christ, and holiness? Why, then, are your hearts so exceedingly raised when the world comes in and smiles upon you, and so much dejected and cast down when the world frowns upon you, and, with Jonah's gourd, withers before you?

THE SERVICE OF GOD.

Christians that would hold on in the service of the Lord, must look more upon the crown than upon the cross, more upon their future glory than their present misery, more upon their encouragements than upon their discouragements. God's very service is wages; his ways are strewed with roses, and paved "with joy that is unspeakable and full of glory," and with "peace that passeth understanding."

UNCERTAIN RICHES.

The Apostle willed Timothy to "charge rich men that they be not high minded, nor put their trust in uncertain riches." They are like bad servants, whose shoes are made of running leather, and will never tarry long with one master. As a bird hoppeth from tree to tree, so do the honours and riches of this world from man to man. Let Job and Nebuchadnezzar testify this truth, who fell from great wealth to great want. No man can promise himself to be wealthy till night: one storm at sea, one coal of fire, one false friend, one unadvised word, one false witness, may make thee a beggar and a prisoner all at once. All the riches and glory of this world are but as smoke and chaff that vanisheth — "As a dream and vision in the night, that tarrieth not." "As if a hungry man dreameth, and thinketh that he eateth, and when he awaketh his soul is empty; and like a thirsty man which thinketh he drinketh, and behold when he is awaked, his soul is faint," as the prophet Isaiah saith. Where is the glory of Solomon? the sumptuous buildings of Nebuchadnezzar? the nine hundred chariots of Sisera? the power of Alexander? the authority of Augustus, that commanded the whole world to be taxed? Those that have been the most glorious, in what men generally account glorious and excellent, have had inglorious ends: as Samson for strength, Absalom for favour, Ahithophel for policy, Haman for favour, Asahel for swiftness, Alexander for great conquest, and yet after twelve years poisoned. The same you may see in the four mighty kingdoms — the Chaldean, Persian, Grecian, and Roman. How soon were they gone and forgotten! Now rich, now poor; now full, now empty; now in favour, anon out of favour; now honourable, now despised; now health, now sickness; now strength, now weakness. Oh, let not these uncertain things keep thee from those holy services and heavenly employments, that may make thee happy forever, and render thy soul eternally blessed and at ease, when all these transitory things shall bid thy soul an everlasting farewell!

THE EVILS OF PROSPERITY.

The great things of this world are very hurtful and dangerous to the outward and inward man, through the corruptions that be in the hearts of men. O the rest, the peace, the comfort, the content that the things of this world do strip many men of! O the fears, the cares, the envy, the malice, the dangers, the mischiefs that they subject men to! They oftentimes make men carnally confident. The rich man's riches are a strong tower in his imagination. "I said in my prosperity I should never be moved." They often swell the heart with pride, and make men forget God, and neglect God, and despise the rock of their salvation. When Jeshurun "waxed fat, and was grown thick, and covered with fatness, then he forgot God, and forsook God that made him, and lightly esteemed the rock of his salvation," as Moses spake. Ah, the time, the thoughts, the spirits, that the things of the world consume and spend! Oh, how do they hinder the actings of faith upon God! how do they interrupt our sweet communion with God! how do they abate our love to the people of God! and cool our love to the things of God! and work us to act like those that are most unlike to God! O the deadness, the barrenness that doth attend men under great outward mercies! O the riches of the world choke the Word! that men live under the most soul-searching and soul-enriching means with lean souls! Though they have full purses, though their chests are full of silver, yet their hearts are empty of grace. In Genesis xiii. 2, it ii said that "Abraham was very rich in cattle, in silver, and in gold." According to the Hebrew, it is, "Abraham was very weary," to show that riches are a heavy burden, and a hindrance many times to heaven and happiness.

LIFE A DREAM.

Man himself is but the dream of a dream, but the generation of a fancy, but an empty vanity, but the curious picture of nothing—a poor, feeble, dying flash. All temporals are as transitory as a hasty headlong current, a shadow, a ship, a bird, an arrow, a post that passeth by.

THE SAINT'S REWARD.

The joy, the rest, the refreshing, the comforts, the contents, the smiles, the incomes that saints now enjoy in the ways of God, are so precious and glorious in their eyes, that they would not exchange them for ten thousand worlds. Ah! if the veils be thus sweet and glorious before payday comes, what will be that glory that Christ will crown his saints with for cleaving to his service in the face of all difficulties; when He shall say to his Father, "Lo, here am I, and the children which thou hast given me?"

AIM HIGH.

He that shooteth at the sun, though he be far short, will shoot higher than he that aimeth at a shrub. It is best, and it speaks out much of Christ within, to eye the highest and the worthiest examples.

Be Humble.

Humility will keep the soul free from many darts of Satan's casting, and erroneous snares of his spreading. As low trees and shrubs are free from many violent gusts and blasts of wind which shake and rend the taller trees, so humble souls are free from those gusts and blasts of error that rend and tear proud, lofty souls. Satan and the world have least power to fasten errors upon humble souls. The God of light and truth delights to dwell with the humble; and the more light and truth dwells in the soul, the further off darkness and error will stand from the soul. The God of grace pours in grace into humble souls, as men pour liquor into empty vessels; and the more grace is poured into the soul, the less error shall be able to overpower the soul, or to infect the soul.

God's Commands.

God's commands are not like those that are easily reversed, but they are like those of the Medes, that cannot be changed. If these commands be not now observed by thee, they will at last be witnesses against thee, and millstones to sink thee, in that day that Christ shall judge thee.

Evil Associations.

How many have lost their names, and lost their estates, and strength, and God, and heaven, and souls, by society with wicked men! As ye shun a stinking carcass, as the seaman shuns sands and rocks, and shoals, as ye shun those that have the plague-sores running upon them,—so should you shun the society of wicked men. As weeds endanger the corn, as bad humours endanger the blood, or as an infected house the neighbourhood, so doth wicked company the soul.

WICKED MEN.

The Scripture calls them lions for their fierceness, and bears for their cruelty, and dragons for their hideousness, and dogs for their filthiness, and wolves for their subtleness. The Scripture styles them scorpions, vipers, thorns, briers, thistles, brambles, stubble, dirt, chaff, dust, dross, and scum. It is not safe to look upon wicked men under those names and notions that they set out themselves by, or that flatterers set them out by. This may delude the soul; but the looking upon them under those names and notions that the Scripture sets them out by, may preserve the soul from frequenting their company and delighting in their society. Do not tell me what this man calls them, or how such and such count them; but tell me how doth the Scripture call them— how doth the Scripture count them? As Nabal's name was, so was his nature; and as wicked men's names are, so are their natures. You may know well enough what is within them, by the apt names that the Holy Ghost hath given them. Guilt or grief is all the good gracious souls get by conversing with wicked men.

RICHES COMPARED TO MANNA.

Riches, though well got, yet are but like to manna; those that gathered less had no want, and those that gathered more, it was but a trouble and annoyance to them. The world is troublesome, and yet it is loved. What would it be if it were peaceable? You embrace it, though it be filthy; what would you do if it were beautiful? You cannot keep your hands from the thorns; how earnest would you be then in gathering the flowers? The world may be fitly likened to the serpent Scytale, whereof it is reported, that when she cannot overtake the flying passengers, she doth with her beautiful colours so astonish and amaze them, that they have no power to pass away, till she hath stung them. Ah, how many thousands are there now on earth, that have found this true by experience, that have spun a fair thread to strangle themselves, both temporally and eternally, by being bewitched by the beauty and bravery of this world.

HUMAN FELICITY.

All the felicity of this world is mixed. Our light is mixed with darkness, our joy with sorrow, our pleasures with pain, our honour with dishonour, our riches with wants. If our lights be spiritual, clear, and quick, we may see in the felicity of this world our wine mixed with water, our honey with gall, our sugar with wormwood, and our roses with prickles. Sorrow attends worldly joy, danger attends worldly safety, loss attends worldly labours, tears attend worldly purposes. As to these things, men's hopes are vain, their sorrows certain, and joy feigned. The Apostle calls this world "a sea of glass," a sea for the trouble of it, and glass for the brittleness and bitterness of it. The honours, profits, pleasures, and delights of the world are true gardens of Adonis, where we can gather nothing but trivial flowers, surrounded with many briers.

LOOK TO HEAVEN.

King Henry the Fourth asked the Duke of Alva if he had observed the great eclipse of the sun, which had lately happened. No, said the Duke, I have so much to do on earth, that I have no leisure to look up to heaven. Ah, that this were not true of most professors in these days! It is very sad to think, how their hearts and time are so much taken up with earthly things, that they have scarce any leisure to look up to heaven, or to look after Christ, and the things that belong to their everlasting peace.

GOODS FOR THE THRONE OF GRACE.

It was an excellent saying of Lewis of Bavyer, Emperor of Germany: "Such goods are worth getting and owning, as will not sink or wash away if a shipwreck happen, but will wade and swim out with us." It is recorded of Lazarus, that after his resurrection from the dead, he was never seen to laugh, his thoughts and affections were so fixed in heaven, though his body was on earth, and therefore he could not but slight temporal things, his heart being so bent and set upon eternals. There are goods for the throne of grace, as God, Christ, the Spirit, adoption, justification, remission of sin, peace with God, and peace with conscience; and there are goods of the footstool, as honours, riches, the favour of creatures, and other comforts and accommodations of this life. Now, he that hath acquaintance with, and assurance of, the goods of the throne, will easily trample upon the goods of the footstool. Ah, that you would make it your business, your work, to mind more, and make sure more to your own souls, the great things of eternity, that will yield you joy in life and peace in death, and a crown of righteousness in the day of Christ's appearing, and that will lift up your souls above all the beauty and bravery of this bewitching world, that will raise your feet above other men's heads!

WHAT IS HAPPINESS?

Happiness lies not in those things that a man may enjoy, and yet be miserable forever. Now, a man may be great and graceless with Pharaoh, honourable and damnable with Saul, rich and miserable with Dives, etc.; therefore happiness lies not in these things that cannot comfort a man upon a dying bed. Is it honours, riches, or friends, etc., that can comfort thee when thou comest to die? Or is it not rather faith in the blood of Christ, the witness of the Spirit of Christ, the sense and feeling of the love and favour of Christ, and the hopes of eternally reigning with Christ? Can happiness lie in those things that cannot give us health, or strength, or ease, or a good night's rest, or an hour's sleep, or a good stomach? Why, all the honours, riches, and delights of this world cannot give these poor things to us; therefore certainly happiness lies not in the enjoyment of them, etc. And surely happiness is not to be found in those things that cannot satisfy the souls of men. Now, none of these things can satisfy the soul of man. "He that loveth silver shall not be satisfied with silver, nor he that loveth abundance with increase; this is also vanity," said the wise man. The barren womb, the horse leech's daughter, the grave and hell, will as soon be satisfied, as the soul of man will by the enjoyment of any worldly good. Some one thing or other will be forever wanting to that soul that hath none but outward good to live upon. You may as soon fill a bag with wisdom, a chest with virtue, or a circle with a triangle, as the heart of man with anything here below. A man may have enough of the world to sink him, but he can never have enough to satisfy him.

Flattery.

Where one thosusand are destroyed by the world's frowns, ten thousand are destroyed by the world's smiles. The world, siren-like, it sings us and sinks us; it kisses us, and betrays us, like Judas; it kisses us and smites us under the fifth rib, like Joab. The honours, splendour, and all the glory of this world, are but sweet poisons, that will much endanger us, if they do not eternally destroy us.

Repent in Time.

What will it be to turn from every sin? Yea, to mortify and cut off those sins, those darling lusts, that are as joints and members—that be as right hands and right eyes? Hast thou not loved thy sins above thy Saviour? Hast thou not preferred earth before heaven? Hast thou not all along neglected the means of grace, and despised the offers of grace, and vexed the Spirit of grace? There would be no end if I should set before thee the infinite evils that thou hast committed, and the innumerable good services that thou hast omitted, and the frequent checks of thy own conscience that thou hast contemned; and therefore thou mayest well conclude that thou canst never repent—that thou shalt never repent. Now, saith Satan, do but a little consider thy numberless sins, and the greatness of thy sins, the foul-ness of thy sins, the heinousness of thy sins, the circumstances of thy sins, and thou shalt easily see that those sins that thou thoughtest to be but motes, are indeed mountains; and is it not now in vain to repent of them? Surely, saith Satan, if thou shouldst seek repentance and grace with tears, as Esau, thou shalt not find it. Thy glass is out, thy sun is set, the door of mercy is shut, the golden sceptre is taken in, and now thou that hast despised mercy, shalt be forever destroyed by justice. For such a wretch as thou art to attempt repentance, is to attempt a thing impossible. It is impossible that thou, that in all thy life couldst never conquer one sin, shouldst master such a numberless number of sins; which are so near, so dear, so necessary, and so profitable to thee; that have so long bedded and boarded with thee; that have been old acquaintance and companions with thee. Hast thou not often purposed, promised, vowed, and resolved to enter upon the practice of repentance, but to this day couldst never attain it? Surely it is in vain to strive against the stream, where it is so impossible to overcome. Thou art lost and cast forever. To hell thou must, to hell thou shalt. Ah, souls! he that now tempts you to sin, by suggesting to you the easiness of repentance, will at last work you to despair, and present repentance as the hardest work in all the world, and a work as far above man as heaven is above hell, as light is above darkness. O that you were wise, to break off your sins by timely repentance!

Flee from Sin.

It is impossible for that man to get the conquest of sin, that plays and sports with the occasions of sin. God will not remove the temptation, except you turn from the occasion. It is a just and righteous thing with God, that he should fall into the pit, that will adventure to dance upon the brink of the pit, and that he should be a slave to sin, that will not flee from the occasions of sin. As long as there is fuel in our hearts for a temptation, we cannot be secure. He that hath gun powder about him had need keep far enough off from sparkles. To rush upon the occasions of sin, is both to tempt ourselves, and to tempt Satan to tempt our souls. It is very rare that any soul plays with the occasions of sin, but that soul is ensnared by sin. It is seldom that God keeps that soul from the acts of sin, that will not keep off from the occasions of sin. He that adventures upon the occasions of sin is as he that would quench the fire with oil, which is a fuel to maintain it, and increase it. Ah, souls I often remember how frequently you have been overcome by sin, when you have boldly gone upon the occasions of sin! Look back, souls, to the day of your vanity, where-in you have been as easily conquered as tempted, van-quished as assaulted, when you have played with the occasions of sin. As you would for the future be kept from the acting of sin, and be made victorious over sin, Oh! flee from the occasions of sin.

CORRUPT NATURE.

The devil counts a fit occasion half a conquest, for he knows that corrupt nature hath a seed-plot for all sin, which, being drawn forth and watered by some sinful occasion, is soon set a-work, to the producing of death and destruction. God will not remove the temptation, till we remove the occasion. A bird whilst aloft is safe, but she comes not near the snare without danger. The shunning the occasions of sin renders a man most like the best of men. A soul eminently gracious, dares not come near the train, though he be far off the blow.

ASPIRATIONS.

It is best and safest to have the eye always fixed upon the highest and noblest objects; as the mariner's eye is fixed upon the star, when his hand is on the stern.

THE JOY OF THE CHRISTIAN.

Let believers live cheerfully and walk comfortably up and down in this world. Ah! how cheerfully and merrily do many great heirs live! Though for the present things go hard with them, the hope of a good inheritance makes them sing care and sorrow away. It is not for the honour of Christ, nor for the glory of the Gospel, to see the heirs of heaven look so sadly and walk so mournfully and dejectedly, as if there were no heaven, or as if there was nothing laid up for them in heaven. It becomes not the sons of glory, with Rachel, to give so much way to weeping as to refuse to be comforted. Dost thou not remember, O Christian, that the joy of the Lord is thy strength, thy doing strength, thy bearing strength, thy prevailing strength. What! hast thou forgotten that "the joy of the Lord is thy strength" to live, and thy strength to die? If not, why with Cain dost thou walk up and down with a dejected countenance, with a cast-down countenance? A beautiful face is at all times pleasing to the eye, but then especially when there is joy manifested in the countenance. Joy in the face puts a new beauty upon a person, and makes that which before was beautiful to be exceedingly beautiful; it puts a new lustre upon beauty; so doth joy put a lustre and a beauty upon a Christian; and upon all his words, his ways, his works. It was this that made the faces of several martyrs to shine as if they had been the faces of angels. One observes of Chispina, that she was cheerful when she was apprehended, and joyful when she was led to the judge, and merry when she was sent into prison; so, when she was bound, when she was brought forth, when she was lifted up in a cage, when she was heard, when she was condemned,—in all these things she rejoiced; so that they who were miserable thought her to be miserable, who indeed was happy under a spirit of joy. When Caesar was sad, he used to say to himself, *Cogita te Caesarem esse*, think thou art Caesar. Ah, Christians! when you are sad and dejected, think of your dignity and glory; think of all those precious and glorious things that are reserved in heaven for you.

THE LOVE OF THE LORD.

The love of the Lord is everlasting; it is a love that never dies, that never decays, nor waxes cold. It is like the stone asbestos, of which Solinus writes, that being once hot, it never can be cooled again. Death is nothing but a bringing of a loving Christ and loving souls together. Why, then, should not the saints rather desire it, than fear it or be dismayed at it?

DEATH THE GATE OF LIFE.

Can death dissolve that glorious union that is between you and Christ? No. Why, why then are you unwilling to die, as long as in death your union with Christ holds good? As in death Saul and Jonathan were not parted, so in death a believer and Christ is not parted, but more closely and firmly united. That is not death, but life, that joins the dying man to Christ; and that is not a life, but death, that separates the living man from Christ. As it is impossible for the leaven that is in the dough to be separated from the dough after it is once mixed, for it turneth the nature of the dough into itself; so it is impossible, either in life or death, for the saints ever to be separated from Christ; for Christ, in respect of union, is in the saints as nearly as the leaven in the very dough,—so incorporated one into another, as if Christ and they wore one lump. Why, why then, O Christian, art thou unwilling to die, as long as the marriage-knot holds fast between Christ and thy soul? I readily grant that death dissolves that marriage-knot that is knit between man and wife; but death nor devil can never dissolve the marriage-knot that is knit between Christ and the believing soul. Sin cannot dissolve that marriage-knot that is knit between Christ and a believer; and if sin cannot, then certainly death, that came in by sin, cannot. Though sin can do more than death, yet sin cannot make null and void that glorious marriage that is between Christ and the soul; therefore a Christian should not be unwilling to die.

AVOID SINFUL OCCASIONS.

The avoiding the occasions of sin, is an evidence of grace, and that which lifts up a man above most other men in the world. That a man is indeed, which he is in temptation; and when sinful occasions do present themselves before the soul, this speaks out both the truth and the strength of grace; when with Lot, a man can be chaste in Sodom, and with Timothy can live temperate in Asia, among the luxurious Ephesians; and with Job can walk uprightly in the land of Uz, where the people were profane in their lives, and superstitious in their worship; and with Daniel be holy in Babylon; and with Abraham righteous in Chaldea; and with Nehemiah, zealous in Damasco, etc. Many a wicked man is big and full of corruption, but shows it not for want of occasion; but that man is surely good, who in his course will not be bad, though tempted by occasions. A Christless soul is so far from refusing occasions when they come in his way, that he looks and longs after them, and rather than he will go without them he will buy them, not only with love or money, but also with the loss of his soul. Nothing but grace can fence a man against the occasions of sin, when he is strongly tempted thereunto. Therefore, as you would cherish a precious evidence in your own bosoms of the truth and strength of your graces, shun all sinful occasions.

ALL THINGS COME ALIKE TO ALL.

No man knoweth either love or hatred by outward mercy or misery; for all things come alike to all, to the righteous and to the unrighteous, to the good and to the bad, to the clean and to the unclean, etc. The sun of prosperity shines as well upon brambles of the wilderness as fruit-trees of the orchard; the snow and hail of adversity lights upon the best garden as well as the stinking dunghill or the wild waste. Ahab's and Josiah's ends concur in the very circumstances. Saul and Jonathan, though different in their natures, deserts, and deportments, yet in their deaths they were not divided. Health, wealth, honours, etc., crosses, sicknesses, losses, etc., are cast upon good men and bad men promiscuously. "The whole Turkish empire is nothing else but a crust, cast by heaven's great housekeeper to his dogs." Moses dies in the wilderness as well as those that murmured. Nabal is rich, as well as Abraham; Ahithophel wise, as well as Solomon; and Doeg honoured by Saul, as well as Joseph was by Pharaoh. Usually the worst of men have most of these outward things; and the best of men have least of earth, though most of heaven.

Look on both Sides.

It is a sad and dangerous thing to have two eyes to behold our dignity and privileges, and not one to see our duties and services. I should look with one eye upon the choice and excellent things that Christ hath done for me, to raise up my heart to love Christ with the purest love, and to joy in Christ with the strongest joy, and to lift up Christ above all, who hath made himself to be my all; and I should look with the other eye upon those services and duties that the Scriptures require of those for whom Christ hath done such blessed things, as upon that of the Apostle: "What, know ye not that your body is the temple of the Holy Ghost, which is in you, which ye have of God? and ye are not your own: for ye are bought with a price; therefore glorify God in your body, and in your spirit, which are God's."

Now, a soul that would not be drawn away by this device of Satan, he must not look with a squint eye upon these blessed Scriptures, and abundance more of like import, but he must dwell upon them; he must make these Scriptures to be his chiefest and his choicest companions, and this will be a happy means to keep him close to Christ and his service in these times, wherein many turn their backs upon Christ, under pretence of being interested in the great glorious things that have been acted by Christ.

Christ's Example.

The great and glorious things that Jesus Christ hath done, and is a-doing for us, should be so far from taking us off from religious services and pious performances, that they should be the greatest motives and encouragements to the performance of them that may be, as the Scriptures do abundantly evidence.

The Mortifying of Sin.

Look upon a rabbit's skin, how well it comes off till it comes to the head, but then what hauling and pulling is there before it stirs! So it is in the mortifying, in the crucifying of sin. A man may easily subdue and mortify such and such sins; but when it comes to the head-sin, to the mastersin, to the bosom-sin, O what tugging and pulling is there, what striving and struggling is there, to get off that sin, to get down that sin! Now, if the Lord, by smiting thee in some near and dear enjoyment, shall draw out thy heart to fall upon smiting of thy master-sin, and shall so sanctify the affliction, as to make it issue in the mortification of thy bosom corruption, what eminent cause wilt thou have rather to bless Him, than to sit down and murmur against Him! And, doubtless, if thou art dear to God, God will, by striking thy dearest mercy, put thee upon striking at thy darling sin; and therefore hold thy peace even then, when God touches the apple of thine eye.

None can Lose by Christ.

The Lord hath many ways to make up the loss of a near and dear mercy to thee. He can make up thy loss in something else that may be better for thee; and He will certainly make up thy loss, either in kind or in worth. He took from David an Absalom, and He gave him a Solomon; He took from him a Michal, and gave him a wise Abigail; He took from Job seven sons and three daughters, and afterwards He gave him seven sons and three daughters; He took from Job a fair estate, and at last doubled it to him; He removed the bodily presence of Christ from his disciples, but gave them more abundantly of his spiritual presence, which was far the greater and the sweeter mercy. If Moses be taken away, Joshua shall be raised in his room; if David be gathered to his fathers, a Solomon shall succeed him in his throne; if John be cast into prison, rather than the pulpit shall stand empty, a greater than John, even Christ himself, will begin to preach. He that lives upon God in the loss of creature comforts, shall find all made up in the God of comforts; he shall be able to say, Though my child is not, my friend is not, my yoke-fellow is not, yet my God liveth, and "blessed be my rock." Though this mercy is not, and that mercy is not, yet covenant-mercies, yet "the sure mercies of David" continue; these bed and board with me; these will [go] to the grave and to glory with me. I have read of a godly man, who, living near a philosopher, did often persuade him to become a Christian. "Oh! but," said the philosopher, "I must, or may, lose all for Christ." To which the good man replied, "If you lose anything for Christ, He will be sure to repay it a hundredfold." "Ay, but," said the philosopher, "will you be bound for Christ, that if He doth not pay me, you will?" "Yes, that I will," said the good man. So the philosopher became a Christian, and the good man entered into bond for performance of covenants. Some time after it happened that the philosopher fell sick on his deathbed, and, holding the bond in his hand, sent for the party engaged, to whom he gave up the bond, and said, "Christ hath paid all; there is nothing for you to pay; take your bond, and cancel it." Christ will suffer none of his children to go by the loss; He hath all, and He will make up all to them. In the close, Christ will pay the reckoning. No man shall ever have cause to say that he hath been a loser by Christ.

THE CHASTENINGS OF LOVE.

Our mercies, like choice wines, many times turn into vinegar; our fairest hopes are often blasted; and that very mercy which we sometimes have said should be a staff to support us, hath proved a sword to pierce us. How often have our most flourishing mercies withered in our hands, and our bosom contentments been turned into gall and wormwood! Many parents who have sought the lives of their children with tears, have lived afterwards to see them take such courses and come to such dismal ends as have brought their grey heads with sorrow to their graves. It had been ten thousand times a greater mercy to many parents to have buried their children so soon as ever they had been born, than to see them come to such unhappy ends as they often do. Well! Christian, it may be the Lord hath taken from thee such a hopeful son, or such a dear daughter, and thou sayest, How can I hold my peace? but hark, Christian, hark! canst thou tell me how long thou must have travailed in birth with them again before they had been twice born? Would not every sin that they had committed against thy gracious God caused a new throe in thy soul? Would not every temptation that they had fallen before been as a dagger at thy heart? Would not every affliction that should have befallen them been as a knife at thy throat? What are those pains, and pangs, and throes of child-birth to those after-pains, pangs, and throes that might have been brought upon thee by the sins and sufferings of thy children? Well! Christians, hold your peace, for you do not know what thorns in your eyes, what goads in your sides, nor what spears in your hearts, such near and dear mercies might have proved had they been longer continued.

THE CHRISTIAN'S TRIALS.

I have read of the pine-tree, that, if the bark be pulled off, it will last a long time; but if it continue long on, it rots the tree. Ah! how bad, how rotten, how base would many have proved, had God not pulled off their bark of health, wealth, friendship! etc. Near and dear relations, they stick as close to us as the bark of a tree; and if God should not pull off this bark, how apt should we be to rot and corrupt ourselves! Therefore God is fain to bark us, and peel us, and strip us naked and bare of our dearest enjoyments and sweetest contentments, that so our souls, like the pine-tree, may prosper and thrive the better. Who can seriously consider of this, and not hold his peace, even then when God takes a jewel out of his bosom? Heap all the sweetest contentments and most desirable enjoyments of this world upon a man, they will not make him a Christian; heap them upon a Christian, they will not make him a better Christian. Many a Christian hath been made worse by the good things of this world; but where is the Christian that hath been bettered by them? Therefore be quiet when God strips thee of them.

THE LOSS OF CHRIST.

I have read of Honorius, a Roman emperor, who was simple and childish enough. When one told him Rome was lost, he was exceedingly grieved, and cried out, Alas, alas! for he supposed that it was his hen that was called Rome, which hen he exceedingly loved; but when it was told him it was his imperial city of Rome that was besieged by Alaricus, and taken, and all the citizens rifled, and made a prey to the rude enraged soldiers, then his spirits were revived that his loss was not so great as he imagined. Now, what is the loss of a husband, a wife, a child, a friend, to the loss of God, Christ, the Spirit, or the least measure of grace or communion with God? etc. I say, What are all such losses, but the loss of a hen to the loss of Rome? And yet so simple and childish are many Christians, that they are more affected and afflicted with the loss of this and that poor temporal enjoyment than they are with the loss of their most spiritual attainments. Ah, Christians! be but more affected with spiritual losses, and you will be more quiet and silent under temporal losses. Let the loss of Rome trouble you more, and then the loss of your hen will not trouble you at all.

CHRIST'S SUFFERING.

Compare thy winter nights and other saints' winter nights together; thy storms and troubles and other saints' storms and troubles together; thy losses and other saints' losses together; thy miseries and other saints' miseries together. Thy afflictions are but as a moment; they are but as yesterday, compared with the afflictions of other saints, whose whole lives have been made up of sorrows and sufferings, as the life of Christ was.

THE GLORY OF HEAVEN.

Long afflictions will much set off the glory of heaven. The harbour is most sweet and desirable to them that have been long tossed upon the seas; so will heaven be to those who have been long in a sea of trouble. The new wine of Christ's kingdom is most sweet to those that have been long a-drinking of gall and vinegar; the crown of glory will be most delightful to them who have been long in combating with the world, the flesh, and the devil. The longer our journey is, the sweeter will be our end, and the longer our passage is, the sweeter will our haven be. The higher the mountain, the gladder we shall be when we are got to the top of it; the longer the heir is kept from his inheritance, the more delight he will have when he comes to possess it.

THE KINGDOM OF HEAVEN.

The kingdoms of this world are not lasting, much less are they everlasting; they have all their climacterical years; but the kingdom of heaven is an everlasting kingdom—of that there is no end. There are seven sorts of crowns that were in use among the Roman victors, but they were all fading and perishing; but the crown of glory that at last God will set upon the heads of his saints, shall continue as long as God himself continues.

EARTHLY PAIN.

Many a man's life hath been nothing but a lingering death. "And another dieth in the bitterness of his soul, and never eateth with pleasure." There are those that have never a good day all their days, who have not a day of rest among all their days of trouble, nor a day of health among all their days of sickness, nor a day of gladness among all their days of sadness, nor a day of strength among all their days of weakness, nor a day of honour among all their days of reproach; whose whole life is one continued winter's night; who every day drink gall and wormwood; who lie down sighing, who rise groaning, and who spend their days in complaining: "No sorrow to our sorrows, no sufferings to our sufferings!" Some there be who have always tears in their eyes, sorrows in their hearts, rods on their backs, and crosses in their hands: but it is not so with the Christian.

THE CHRISTIAN'S AFFLICTION.

The afflicted Christian's heart is fullest of spiritual treasure. Though he may be poor in the world, yet he is rich in faith and holy experiences; and what are all the riches of this world to spiritual experiences? One spiritual experience is more worth than a world; and upon a dying bed and before a judgment-seat, every man will be of this opinion. The men of this world will, with much quietness and calmness of spirit, bear much, and suffer much, and suffer long, when they find their sufferings to add to their revenues; and shall nature do more than grace? It is the common voice of nature, "Who will show us any good?" How shall we come to be great, and high, and rich in the world? We care not what we suffer, nor how long we suffer, so we may but add house to house, heap to heap, bag to bag, and land to land. Oh, how much more, then, should Christians be quiet and calm under all their afflictions, though they are never so long, considering that they do but add jewels to a Christian's crown! they do but add to his spiritual experiences. The long afflicted Christian hath the fullest and the greatest trade; and, in the day of account, will be found the richest man.

GRACE AND GLORY.

The more grace here, the more glory hereafter; the higher in grace, the higher in glory. Grace differs nothing from glory but in name; grace is glory in the bud, and glory is grace at the full. Glory is nothing but the perfection of grace; happiness is nothing but the perfection of holiness. Grace is glory in the seed, and glory is grace in the flower; grace is glory militant, and glory is grace triumphant.

CONFORMITY TO CHRIST.

It is one of God's great designs and ends in afflicting his people, to make them more conformable to his Son; and God will not lose his end. Men often lose theirs, but God never hath nor will lose his; and experience tells us that God doth every day, by afflictions, accomplish his end upon his people. The longer they are afflicted, the more they are made conformable to Christ in meekness, lowliness, spiritualness, heavenliness, in faith, love, self-denial, pity, compassion, etc. Now, certainly, the more like to Christ, the more beloved of Christ. The more a Christian is like to Christ, the more he is the delight of Christ; and the more like to Christ on earth, the nearer the soul shall sit to Christ in heaven.

CHRISTIAN FORBEARANCE.

Impatience will but lengthen out the day of thy sorrows. Every impatient act adds one link more to the chain; every act of frowardness adds one lash more to those that have already been laid out; every act of muttering will but add stroke to stroke, and sting to sting; every act of murmuring will but add burden to burden, and storm to storm. The most compendious way to lengthen out thy long afflictions is to fret, and vex, and murmur under them. As thou wouldst see a speedy issue of thy long afflictions, sit mute and silent under them.

"NOW" IS THE TIME.

The past cannot be recalled, and time to come cannot be ascertained: "Today, if you hear his voice, harden not your hearts:" "Behold, now is the accepted time, now is the day of salvation." Some there be that trifle away their time, and fool away their souls and their salvation. To prevent this, the Apostle beats upon the present opportunity, because if that be once past, there is no recovering of it. Therefore, as the mariner takes the first fair wind to sail, and as the merchant takes his first opportunity of buying and selling, and as the husbandman takes the first opportunity of sowing and reaping, so should young men take the present season, the present day, which is their day, to be good towards the Lord, to seek Him and serve Him, and not to post off the present season, for they know not what another day, another hour, another moment, may bring forth. That door of grace that is open today may be shut to-morrow; that golden sceptre of mercy that is held forth in the Gospel this day may be taken in the next day; that love that this hour is upon the bare knee entreating and beseeching young men to break off their sins by repentance, "to return to the Lord, to lay hold on his strength, and be at peace with Him," may the next hour be turned into wrath.

The Present Time Only Our Own.

There is no time yours but the present time, no day yours but the present day; and therefore do not please yourselves and feed yourselves with hopes of time to come, and that you will repent, but not yet, and lay hold on mercy, but not yet, and give up yourselves to the Lord next week, next month, or next year; for that God that hath promised you mercy and favour upon the day of your return, He hath not promised to prolong your lives till that day comes. When a soldier was brought before Lamacus, a commander, for a misbehaviour, and pleaded he would do so no more, Lamacus answered, "No man must offend twice in war." So God, especial-ly in these Gospel-days, wherein the motions of Divine justice are more smart and quick than in former days, happily will not suffer men twice to neglect the day of grace, and let slip the season of mercy.

A Three-Word Repentance.

I have read of a certain young man, who, being admon-ished of the evil of his way and course, and pressed to leave his wickedness by the consideration of death, judgment, and eternity, that was a-coming, he answered,—What do you tell me of these things? I will do well enough; for when death comes, I will speak but three words, and will help all; and so still he went on in his sinful ways, but in the end, coming to a bridge on horseback, to go over a deep water, the horse stumbling, and he labouring to recover his horse, but could not. At last, he let go the bridle, and gave up himself and horse to the waters, and was heard to say these three words, Devil take all, *Diabolus capiat omnia!* Here were three dreadful words indeed, and an example, with a witness, for all young men to beware who think to repent with a three-word repentance at last.

Soul-Opportunities.

How many, for slipping gracious seasons and opportunities, have died forever! Soul-opportunities are more worth than a thousand worlds; mercy is in them, grace and glory are in them, heaven and eternity are in them.

Do Not put off God.

Do not put off God to old age; for old, lame, and sick sacrifices rarely reach as high as heaven. Is not old age very unteachable? In old age are not men very unapt to take in, and as unapt to give out? In old age, oftentimes, men are men, and no men: they have eyes, but see not; ears, but hear not; tongues, but speak not; feet, but walk not. An aged man is but a moving anatomy, or a living mortuary. Now, how unlovely, how uncomely, how unworthy, nay, how incensing, how provoking a thing must this needs be, when men will dally with God, and put Him off till their doating days have overtaken them; till their spring is past, their summer overpast, and they arrived at the fall of the leaf; yea, till winter colours have stained their heads with grey and hoary hairs! How provoking this is, you may see in those sad words of Jeremiah: "I spake unto thee in thy prosperity; but thou saidst, I will not hear: this hath been thy manner from thy youth, that thou obeyest not my voice." But will God put up with this at their hands? No. Therefore it follows in the next verse, "Surely thou shalt be ashamed and confounded for all thy wickedness."

The Work and the Reward.

Man's wages, man's reward, shall be according to his works. He that doth most work here shall have most reward hereafter. God will at last proportion the one to the other, the reward to the work: "He which soweth sparingly shall reap sparingly; and he which soweth bountifully shall reap bountifully." Though no man shall be rewarded *for* his works, yet God will at last measure out happiness and blessedness to his people *according to* their service, faithfulness, diligence, and work in this world.

Good Work.

"No man can commend good works magnificently enough," saith Luther, "for one work of a Christian is more precious than heaven and earth; and therefore all the world cannot sufficiently reward one good work." And in another place, saith the same author, "If I might have my desire, I would rather choose the meanest work of a country Christian, or poor maid, than all the victories and triumphs of Alexander the Great, and of Julius Ceasar."

MERE PROFESSION WORTHLESS.

As the phoenix in Arabia gathers sweet odoriferous sticks together, and then blows them with her wings, and burns herself with them, so many a carnal professor burns himself with his own good works, that is, by his expecting and trusting to receive that by his works that is only to be received and expected from Jesus Christ. Though all that man can do towards the meriting of heaven is no more than the lifting up of a straw towards the meriting of a kingdom, yet such a proud piece man is, that he is ready enough to say with proud Vega, I will not have heaven of free cost. A proud heart would fain have that of debt which is merely of grace, and desires that to be of purchase which God hath intended to be of free mercy; which made one to say, that he would swim through a sea of brimstone that he might come to heaven at last; but he that swims not thither through the sea of Christ's blood, shall never come there. Man must swim thither, not through brimstone, but through blood, or he miscarries forever.

THE POWER OF GRACE.

The sooner a man begins to be gracious, the sooner and the more useful will his arts, his parts, his gifts, his graces, his mercies, his experiences, his life, his labours, his prayers, his counsels, his examples, be to all that are with him, to all that are about him.

Be Good Betimes.

Ah! young men, young men! as you would be useful and serviceable to many, begin to be good betimes, and to lay in and lay up and lay out betimes, for the profit and advantage of others. Augustine accounted nothing his own that he did not communicate to others. The bee doth store her hive out of all sorts of flowers for the common benefit. It is a base and unworthy spirit for a man to make himself the centre of all his actions. The very heathen man could say that a man's country, and his friends, and others, challenge a great part of him. And indeed the best way to do ourselves good is to be a-doing good to others; the best way to gather is to scatter. Memorable is that story of Pyrrhias, a merchant of Ithaca, who, at sea, espying an aged man, a captive in a pirate's ship, took compassion of him, and redeemed him, and bought his commodities which the pirate had taken from him, which were certain barrels of pitch. The old man perceiving that not for any good service he could do him, nor for the gain of that commodity, but merely out of charity and pity he had done this, discovered a great mass of treasure hidden in the pitch, whereby the merchant in a very short time became very rich; at which very time God made that word good, "He that soweth liberally shall reap liberally;" and that word, "The liberal soul shall be made fat;" and that word, "The liberal deviseth liberal things, and by liberal things shall he stand." It is fabled of Midas, that whatever he touched he turned it into gold. It is certain that a liberal hand, a liberal heart, turns all into gold, into gain, as Scripture and experience do abundantly evidence. Now, if you put all these things together, nothing is more evident than that those that begin to be good betimes are in the ready way, the high way, to be high in heaven when they shall cease from breathing on earth. And therefore, young men, as you would be high in heaven, as you would have a great reward, a full reward, a massy, weighty crown, O labour to be good betimes; labour to get acquainted with the Lord, and an interest in the Lord, in the spring and morning of your days!

Turn to Christ Now.

Early turning to the Lord will prevent many temptations to despair, many temptations to neglect the means openly, to despise the means secretly; many temptations about the being of God, the goodness, faithfulness, truth, and justice of God; temptations to despair, temptations to lay violent hands on a man's self. Temptations to question all that God hath said, and that Christ hath suffered, arise many times from men's delaying and putting off of God to the last; all which, with many others, are prevented by a man's seeking and serving of the Lord in the spring and morning of his youth. It is reported of the harts of Scythia, that they teach their young ones to leap from bank to bank, from rock to rock, from one turf to another, by leaping before them, by which means, when they are hunted, no beast of prey can ever take them; so, when persons exercise themselves in godliness when they are young, when they leap from one measure of holiness to another, when they are in the morning of their days, Satan, that mighty hunter after souls, may pursue them with his temptations; but he shall not overtake them, he shall not prevail over them.

SAVE THY SOUL.

Do not pawn your souls, do not sell your souls, do not exchange away your souls, do not trifle and fool away your precious souls; they are jewels, more worth than a thousand worlds, yea, than heaven and earth. If they are safe, all is safe; but if they are lost, all is lost: God lost, and Christ lost, and the society of glorious angels and blessed saints lost, and heaven lost, and that forever.

Granetensis tells of a woman that was so affected with souls' miscarryings, that she besought God to stop up the passage into hell with her soul and body, that none might have entrance. Ah! that all were so affected with the worth and excellency of their souls, and so alarmed with the hazard and danger of losing their souls, as that they may, in the spring and morning of their days, inquire after the Lord, and seek Him, and serve Him with all their might, that so their precious and immortal souls may be safe and happy forever.

THE DAY OF DEATH.

I have read a remarkable story of a king that was heavy and sad, and wept, which, when his brother saw, he asked him why he was so pensive? Because, saith he, I have judged others, and now I must be judged myself. And why, saith his brother, do you so take on for this? It will, happily, be a long time ere that day come, and besides that, it is but a slight matter. The king said little to it for the present. Now, it was a custom in that country, when any man had committed treason, there was a trumpet sounded at his door in the night time, and he was next day brought out to be executed. Now, the king commanded a trumpet to be sounded at his brother's door in the night-time, who, awakening out of his sleep, when he heard it, arose, and came quaking and trembling to the king. How now? saith the king; what's the matter you are so affrighted? I am, saith he, attached of treason, and next morning I shall be executed. Why, saith the king to him again, are you so troubled at that, knowing that you shall be judged by your brother, and for a matter that your conscience tells you you are clear of? How much more, therefore, may I be afraid, seeing that God shall judge me, and not in a matter that my conscience frees me of, but of that whereof I am guilty? And, beside this, if the worst come, it is but a temporary death you shall die; but I am liable to death eternal, both of body and soul. I will leave the application to those persons that put this day afar off, and whom no arguments will move to be good betimes, and to acquaint themselves with the Lord in the morning of their youth.

WHAT CHRIST DID FOR SOULS.

A soul is a spiritual, immortal substance: it is capable of the knowledge of God, it is capable of union with God, of communion with God, and of a blessed and happy fruition of God. Christ left his Father's bosom for the good of souls; He assumed man's nature for the salvation of man's soul. Christ prayed for souls, He sweat for souls, He wept for souls, He bled for souls, He hung on the cross for souls, He trod the wine-press of his Father's wrath for souls, He died for souls, He rose again from death for souls, He ascended for souls, He intercedes for souls, and all the glorious preparations that He hath been a-making in heaven these sixteen hundred years is for souls.

THE DAY OF JUDGMENT.

To those who begin to seek, serve, and love the Lord in the primrose of their days, the day of judgment will be to them *melodia in aure, jubilum in corde,* like music in the ear, and a jubilee in the heart. This day will be to them a "day of refreshing, a day of redemption," a day of vindication, a day of coronation, a day of consolation, a day of salvation; it will be to them a marriage-day, a harvest-day, a pay-day. Now the Lord will pay them for all the prayers they have made, for all the sermons they have heard, for all the tears they have shed. In this great day Christ will remember all the individual offices of love and friendship shown to any of his. Now He will mention many things for their honour and comfort that they never minded. Now the least and lowest acts of love and pity towards his shall be interpreted as a special kindness shown to himself. Now the crown shall be set upon their heads, and the royal robes put upon their backs. Now all the world shall see that they have not served the Lord for nought. Now Christ will pass over all their weaknesses, and make honourable mention of all the services they have performed, of all the mercies they have improved, and of all the great things that for his name and glory they have suffered.

WISE IN GOD'S SIGHT.

In all ages God hath had some that have been great, rich, wise, and honourable, that have chosen his ways, and cleaved to his service in the face of all difficulties. Though not many wise men, yet some wise men; and though not many mighty, yet some mighty have; and though not many noble, yet some noble have. Witness

Abraham, and Jacob, and Job, and several kings, and others that the Scriptures speak of. And, Ah! how many have we among ourselves, whose souls have cleaved to the Lord, and who have swum to his service through the blood of the slain, and who have not counted their lives dear unto them, that they and others might enjoy the holy things of Christ, according to the mind and heart of Christ.

MUCH IN HOPE.

Though saints have little in hand, yet they have much in hope. You count those happy, in a worldly sense, that have much in reversion, though they have little in possession; and will you count the saints miserable because they have little in hand, little in possession, though they have a glorious kingdom in reversion of this? I am sure the poorest saint that breathes will not exchange, were it in his power, that which he hath in hope and in reversion, for the possession of as many worlds as there be stars in heaven, or sands in the sea.

SPIRITUAL RICHES.

The spiritual riches of the poorest saints do infinitely transcend the temporal riches of all the wicked men in the world; their spiritual riches do satisfy them; they can sit down satisfied with riches of grace that be in Christ, without honours, and without riches. "He that drinks of that water that I shall give him, shall thirst no more." The riches of poor saints are durable; they will bed and board with them; they will go to the prison, to a sick-bed, to a grave, yea, to heaven with them. The spiritual riches of poor saints are as wine to cheer them, and as bread to strengthen them, and as cloth to warm them, and as armour to protect them.

The Number of the Saints.

Though the saints, considered comparatively, are few; though they be a "little, little flock," a "remnant," "a garden enclosed," "a spring shut up, a fountain sealed;" though they are as "the summer gleanings;" though they are one "of a city, and two of a tribe;" though they be but a handful to a houseful, a spark to a flame, a drop to the ocean, yet, consider them simply in themselves, and so they are an innumerable number that cannot be numbered.

God's School.

Temptation is God's school, wherein He gives his people the clearest and sweetest discoveries of his love; a school wherein God teaches his people to be more frequent and fervent in duty,—when Paul was buffeted, then he prayed thrice, *i.e.,* frequently and fervently; a school wherein God teaches his people to be more tender, meek, and compassionate to other poor, tempted souls than ever; a school wherein God teaches his people to see a greater evil in sin than ever, and a greater emptiness in the creature than ever, and a greater need of Christ and free grace than ever; a school wherein God will teach his people that all temptations are but his goldsmiths, by which He will try and refine, and make his people more bright and glorious. The issue of all temptations shall be to the good of the saints, as you may see by the temptations that Adam and Eve, and Christ and David, and Job and Peter and Paul met with.

Those hands of power and love that bring light out of darkness, good out of evil, sweet out of bitter, life out of death, heaven out of hell, will bring much sweet and good to his people, out of all the temptations that come upon them.

WHO BLOTTETH OUT OUR TRANSGRESSIONS?

Who is this that blots out transgressions? He that hath the keys of heaven and hell at his girdle, that opens and no man shuts, that shuts and no man opens; He that hath the power of life and death, of condemning and absolving, of killing and making alive,—He it is that blots out transgressions. If an under-officer should blot out an indictment, that perhaps might do a man no good, a man might for all that be at last cast by the judge; but when the judge or king shall blot out the indictment with their own hand, then the indictment cannot return. Now this is every believer's case and happiness.

THE MALICE OF SATAN.

Satan is a malicious and envious enemy. As his names are, so is he. His names are all names of enmity: the accuser, the tempter, the destroyer, the devourer, the envious man. And this malice and envy of his he shows sometimes by tempting men to such sins as are quite contrary to the temperature of their bodies, as he did Vespasian and Julian—men of sweet and excellent natures—to be most bloody murderers. And sometimes he shows his malice by tempting men to such things as will bring them no honour nor profit; and sometimes he shows his malice by tempting them to those sins which they have not found their natures prone to, and which they abhor in others. Now, if the soul resists these, and complains of these, and groans and mourns under these, and looks up to the Lord Jesus to be delivered from these, then shall they not be put down to the soul's account, but to Satan's, who shall be so much the more tormented, by how much the more the saints have been by him maliciously tempted.

Make present and peremptory resistance against Satan's temptations; bid defiance to the temptation at first sight. It is safe to resist, it is dangerous to dispute. Eve lost herself and her posterity by falling into lists of dispute, when she should have resisted, and stood upon terms of defiance with Satan. He that would stand in the hour of temptation must plead with Christ, "It is written." He that would triumph over temptations must plead still, "It is written." Satan is bold and impudent, and if you are not peremptory in your resistance, he will give you fresh onsets. It is your greatest honour, and your highest wisdom, peremptorily to withstand the beginnings of a temptation, for an after-remedy comes often too late.

Mrs Catherine Bretterege once, after a great conflict with Satan, said, "Reason not with me; I am but a weak woman; if thou hast anything to say, say it to my Christ; He is my advocate, my strength, and my Redeemer, and He shall plead for me."

Men must not seek to resist Satan's craft with craft, but by open defiance. He shoots with Satan in his own bow, who thinks by disputing and reasoning to put him off. As soon as a temptation shows its face, say to the temptation, as Ephraim to his idols, "Get you hence; what have I any more to do with you?" Oh, say to the temptation, as David said to the sons of Zeruiah, "What have I to do with you?" You will be too hard for me. He that doth thus resist temptations, shall never be undone by temptations.

THE FAITHFUL PROMISER.

Antiochus promised often, but seldom gave; upon which he was called, in way of derision, a great promiser; but Jesus Christ never made any promise but He hath or will perform it; nay, He is often better than his word; He gives many times more than we ask. The sick man of the palsy asked but health, and Christ gave him health and pardon to boot. Solomon desired but wisdom, and the Lord gave him wisdom, and honour, and riches, and the favour of creatures as paper and packthread into the bargain. Jacob asked Him but clothes to wear, and bread to eat, and the Lord gave him these things, and riches, and other mercies into the bargain. Christ doth not measure his gifts by our petitions, but by his own riches and mercies. Gracious souls many times receive many gifts and favours from God that they never dreamt of, nor durst presume to beg, which others extremely strive after and go without.

THE TEMPTATIONS OF THE SAINTS.

Those that have been best and most beloved have been most tempted by Satan. Though Satan can never rob a Christian of his crown, yet such is his malice, that he will therefore tempt, that he may spoil them of their comforts. Such is his enmity to the Father, that the nearer and dearer any child is to Him, the more will Satan trouble him, and vex him with temptations. Christ himself was most near and most dear, most innocent and most excellent, and yet none so much tempted as Christ. David was dearly beloved, and yet by Satan tempted to number the people. Job was highly praised by God himself, and yet much tempted; witness those sad things that fell from his mouth, when he was wet to the skin. Peter was much prized by Christ; witness that choice testimony that Christ gave of his faith and happiness, and his showing him his glory in the Mount, and that eye of pity that He cast upon him after his fearful fall, etc., and yet tempted by Satan. "And the Lord said, Simon, Simon, behold, Satan hath desired to have you, that he may sift you as wheat! but I have prayed for thee, that thy faith fail thee not." Paul had the honour of being exalted as high as heaven, and of seeing that glory that could not be expressed; and yet he was no sooner stepped out of heaven, but he is buffeted by Satan, "lest he should be exalted above measure." If these, that were so really, so gloriously, so eminently beloved of God, if these that have lived in heaven, and set their feet upon the stars, have been tempted, let no saints judge themselves not to be beloved because they are tempted. It is as natural for saints to be tempted, that are dearly beloved, as it is for the sun to shine, or a bird to sing. The eagle complains not of her wings, nor the peacock of his train, nor the nightingale of her voice, because these are natural to them; no more should saints of their temptations, because they are natural to them. "For we wrestle not against flesh and blood, but against principalities, against powers, against the rulers of the darkness of this world, against spiritual wickedness in high places.

CHRISTIAN CONFERENCE.

The Jews have a proverb, that two dry sticks put to a green one will kindle it. The best way to be in a flame God-ward, Christ-ward, heaven-ward, and holiness-ward, is to be among the dry sticks, the kindle-coals, the saints; for as live coals kindle those that are dead, so lively Christians will heat and enliven those that are dead God-wards, Christ-wards, heaven-wards, and holiness-wards. "As iron sharpeneth iron, so doth the face of a man his friend." Men's wits, parts, and gifts, and industry, commonly grow more strong, vigorous, and quick, by friendly conference and communion. And as he that comes where sweet spices and ointments are stirring, carries away a sweet savour with him, so he that converseth with those that are good shall carry away that goodness and sweetness with him that shall render him sweet, desirable, and delectable to others. Dr Taylor, the martyr, rejoiced that ever he came into prison, because he came thither to have acquaintance with that angel of God, John Bradford, as he calls him; so, doubtless, many young persons there be that have much cause to rejoice, and forever to bless the Lord, that ever they came acquainted with such and such who fear the Lord, and who walk in his ways, for the good that they have received by them.

AVOID SIN.

Shun the occasions of sin betimes. A man will never begin to be good till he begin to decline those occasions that have made him bad. "Abstain from all appearance of evil." You must shun and be shy of the very appearance of sin, of the very shows and shadows of sin. "Abstain from all sort, or the whole kind of evil;" from all that is truly so, be it never so small. The least sin is dangerous. Caesar was stabbed with bodkins, and many have been eaten up of mice and lice. The least spark may consume the greatest house; the least leak may sink the greatest ship; the least sin is enough to undo thy soul; and therefore shun all the occasions that lead unto it. Job made a covenant with his eyes; Joseph would not be in the room where his mistress was; and David, when himself, would not sit with vain persons. As long as there is fuel in our hearts for a temptation, we cannot be secure; he that hath gunpowder about him, had need keep far enough off from sparkles; he that is either tender of his credit abroad, or comfort at home, had need shun and be shy of the very show and shadow of sin; he that would neither wound conscience nor credit, God nor Gospel, had need hate "the garment spotted with the flesh."

THE VOICE OF CONSCIENCE.

A man will never begin to be good till he begins to hearken to what conscience speaks. So long as a man turns a deaf ear to conscience, he is a safe prisoner to Satan, and a sure enemy to good. Ah! how good might many have been had they but begun betimes to hearken to conscience! Do not dally with conscience; do not play, do not trifle with conscience; do not stop your ears against conscience. He that will not in his youth give conscience audience, shall at last be forced to hear such lectures from conscience, as shall make his life a very hell. A sleepy conscience is like a sleepy lion,—when he awakes, he roars and tears; so will conscience. Conscience is a thousand witnesses for or against a man.

A QUIET SPIRIT.

A quiet, silent spirit is of great esteem with God. God sets the greatest value upon persons of a quiet spirit. "But let it be the hidden man of the heart, in that which is not corruptible, even the ornament of a meek and quiet spirit, which is in the sight of God of great price." A quiet spirit is a spark of the Divine nature; it is a ray, a beam of glory; it is a heaven-born spirit. No man is born with a holy silence in his heart, as he is born with a tongue in his mouth. This is a flower of Paradise; it is a precious gem that God makes very great reckoning of. A quiet spirit speaks a man most like to God; it capacitates a man for communion with God; it renders a man most serviceable to God; and it obliges a man to most accurate walking with God. A meek and quiet spirit is an incorruptible ornament, much more valuable than gold.

THE WILL OF GOD.

How often have you prayed that the will of God may be done, yea, that it may be done on the earth, as the angels, those glistering courtiers, those princes of glory, do it now in heaven! When troubles and afflictions come upon you, the will of God is done—his will is accomplished. Why, then, should you fret, fling, and fume, and not rather quietly lie down in his will, whose will is a perfect will, a just and righteous will, a wise will, an overruling will, an infinite will, a sovereign will, a holy will, an immutable will, an uncontrollable will, an omnipotent will, and an eternal will? Certainly you will but add affliction to affliction, by fighting against your own prayers, and by vexing and fretting yourselves when the will of God is done. It is sad to see a man fight against his friends; it is sadder to see him fight against his relations; it is saddest of all to see him fight against his prayers; and yet this every Christian doth who murmurs and mutters when the rod of God is upon him.

Flee from Evil.

It is a greater miracle not to fall, being among strong occasions, than it is to raise up the dead. He that would not be defiled, must not touch pitch; he that would not be burnt, must not carry fire in his bosom; he that would not eat the meat, must not meddle with the broth; he that would not fall into the pit, must not dance upon the brink; he that would not feel the blow, must keep off from the train: "Keep thee for from a false matter." He that will not fly from the occasions and allurements of sin, though they may seem never so pleasant to the eye, or sweet to the taste, shall find them in the end more sharp than vinegar, more bitter than wormwood, more deadly than poison.

God's Chastening.

The bee sucks sweet honey out of the bitterest herbs; so God will by afflictions teach his children to suck sweet knowledge, sweet obedience, and sweet experiences, out of all the bitter afflictions and trials He exercises them with. That scouring and rubbing, which frets others, shall make them shine the brighter; and that weight which crushes and keeps others under, shall but make them, like the palm-tree, grow better and higher; and that hammer which knocks others all in pieces, shall but knock them the nearer to Christ, the corner-stone. Stars shine brightest in the darkest night; torches give the best light when beaten; grapes yield most wine when most pressed; spices smell sweetest when pounded; vines are the better for bleeding; gold looks the brighter for scouring; juniper smells sweetest in the fire; camomile, the more you tread it the more you spread it; the salamander lives best in the fire; the Jews were best when most afflicted; the Athenians would never mend till they were in mourning; the Christ's cross, saith Luther, is no letter in the book, and yet, saith he, it hath taught me more than all the letters in the book. Afflictions are the saint's best benefactors to heavenly affections; where afflictions hang heaviest, corruptions hang loosest. And grace that is bid in nature, as sweet water in rose leaves, is then most fragrant when the fire of affliction is put under to distil it out. Grace shines the brighter for scouring, and is most glorious when it is most clouded.

THE TRIALS OF CHRIST.

When Christ was young, He was tempted and tried; when He was in the morning of his days, his wounds were deep, his burden weighty, his cup bitter, his sweat painful, his agony and torment above conception, beyond expression; when He was young, that blessed head of his was crowned with thorns; and those eyes of his, that were purer than the sun, were put out by the darkness of death; and those ears of his, which now hear nothing but hallelujahs of saints and angels, were filled with the blasphemies of the multitude; and that blessed, beautiful face of his, which was fairer than the sons of men, was spit on by beastly, filthy wretches; and that gracious mouth and tongue, that spake as never man spake, was slandered and accused of blasphemy; and those hands of his, which healed the sick, which gave out pardons, which swayed a sceptre in heaven, and another on earth, were nailed to the cross; and those feet, that were beautiful upon the mountains, that brought the glad tidings of peace and salvation into the world, and that were like unto fine brass, were also nailed to the cross; all these great and sad things did Jesus suffer for you in the prime and flower of his days; and oh! what an unspeakable provocation should this be to all young ones, to give up themselves betimes to Christ,—to serve, love, honour, and obey Him betimes, even in the spring and morning of their youth. "Let the thoughts of a crucified Christ," saith one, "be never out of your mind; let them be meat and drink unto you; let them be your sweetness and consolation, your honey and your desire, your reading and your meditation, your life, death, and resurrection."

CHRISTIAN FRIENDSHIP.

Man is made to be a friend, and apt for friendly offices. He that is not friendly is not worthy to have a friend; and he that hath a friend, and doth not show himself friendly, is not worthy to be accounted a man. Friendship is a kind of life, without which there is no comfort of a man's life. Christian friendship ties such a knot that great Alexander cannot cut. Summer friends I value not, but winter friends are worth their weight in gold; and who can deny such anything, especially in these days, wherein real, faithful, constant friends are so rare to be found? The friendship of most men in these days is like Jonah's gourd, now very promising and flourishing, and anon fading and withering; it is like some plants in the water, which have broad leaves on the surface of the water, but scarce any root at all; their friendship is like melons, cold within, hot without; their expressions are high, but their affections are low; they speak much, but do little. As drums and trumpets and ensigns in a battle make a great noise and a fine show, but act nothing, so these counterfeit friends will compliment highly, bow handsomely, speak plausibly, and promise lustily, and yet have neither a hand nor heart to act anything cordially or faithfully. From such friends it is a mercy to be delivered, and therefore King Antigonus was wont to pray to God that He would protect him from his friends; and when one of his council asked him why he prayed so, he returned this answer, "Every man will shun and defend himself against his professed enemies; but from our professed or pretended friends, of whom few are faithful, none can safeguard himself, but hath need of protection from Heaven." But for all this, there are some that are real friends, faithful friends, active friends, winter friends, bosom friends, fast friends; and for their sakes, especially those among them that have been long, very long, under the smarting rod, and in the fiery furnace, and that have been often poured from vessel to vessel, have I once more appeared in print to the world.

READING AND APPLICATION.

Reading is but the drawing of the bow; application is the hitting of the white. The choicest truths will no further profit you than they are applied by you; you were as good not to read, as not to apply what you read. No man attains to health by reading of Galen, or knowing Hippocrates' aphorisms, but by the practical application of them. All the reading in the world will never make for the health of your souls, except you apply what you read. The true reason why many read so much and profit so little, is because they do not apply and bring home what they read to their own souls.

Growth in Grace.

As he that sets up for himself betimes is in the most hopeful way to be rich betimes, so he that is good in good earnest betimes, he is in the ready way, the highway of being rich in grace and rich in goodness. They usually prove men of great observation and great experience. God loves to show these his "beauty and his glory in his sanctuary." He delights to cause "his glory and his goodness to pass before" such. These shall find all his "paths drop marrow and fatness." For these "the Lord of hosts will make a feast of fat things, a feast of wines on the lees, of fat things full of marrow, of wines on the lees well refined." These shall have all manner of "pleasant fruits" laid up "at their gates for their well-beloved." None have so many choice pledges of Christ's love, nor so many sweet kisses of Christ's mouth, nor so many embraces in Christ's arms, as those souls that are good betimes. O the grace, the goodness, the sweetness, the fatness that Christ is still a-dropping into their hearts! Christ will make their hearts his largest treasury; He will lay up most of his heavenly treasure in their souls. There He will store up mercies new and old; there He will treasure up all plenty, rarity, and variety; there He will lay up all that heart can wish or need require.

THE NOBILITY OF GRACE.

Grace doth not destroy nature, but rather perfect it. Grace is of a noble offspring; it neither turneth men into stocks nor to stoics. The more grace, the more sensible of the tokens, frowns, blows, and lashes of a displeased Father. Though Calvin, under his greatest pains, was never heard to mutter nor murmur, yet he was heard often to say, "How long, Lord, how long?" A religious commander being shot in battle, when the wound was searched, and the bullet cut out, some standing by, pitying his pain, he replied, "Though I groan, yet I bless God I do not grumble."

LOOK TO HEAVEN.

Galen speaks of a fish called the heaven gazer, which hath but one eye, and that is so placed that it is always looking upwards towards heaven; and so should a Christian's eye of hope be always fixed on God, on promises, on heaven, on the inheritance of the saints in light, and on all those precious and glorious things that are laid up for them in that royal palace where Christ is all in all.

GOD'S PRESENCE.

No man in this world hath so complete and full a presence of God, but he may have a fuller; but in heaven the presence of God shall be so full and complete, as that nothing can be added to it to make it more complete. Sometimes sin, sometimes Satan, sometimes the world, sometimes resting in duties, sometimes the weakness of our graces, hinder us from enjoying a full presence of God here; but in heaven there shall be nothing to interpose between God and us; there shall be nothing to hinder us from enjoying a full and complete presence of God. It is this full presence of God that is the heaven of heaven, the glory of all our glory. An imperfect and incomplete presence of God in heaven would darken all the glory of that state. It is the full and perfect presence of God in heaven that is the most sparkling diamond in the ring of glory; and this you shall have.

The Christian's Desire.

How do the heirs of this world long to have their estates in their own hands? how do they long to have their inheritances settled upon them! some of them wishing their relations dead that stand between them and their inheritances; and others, of a little better nature, wishing them in the bosom of Abraham, that they might come to inherit, and that they might suck the sweet, and take up their rest, in their worldly inheritances. And shall not the saints desire and long to be in a full and happy possession of that crown, of that inheritance, of those jewels that are reserved in heaven for them? O Christians! how is it, why is it, that your heavenly Jerusalem, your mansions above, your glorious treasures, suffer not an holy violence, in respect of your earnest wishes and burning desires after them?

A Christian's Motto.

A Christian's motto always is, or always should be, *Spero meliora*, I hope for better things; I hope for better things than any the world can give to me, or than any that Satan can take from me. A Christian is always rich in hope, though he hath not always a penny in hand.

in hope, though he hath not always a penny in hand.

www.ingramcontent.com/pod-product-compliance
Lightning Source LLC
Chambersburg PA
CBHW011936050726

47590CB00011B/3319